Kidnapped!

A LIVING NIGHTMARE

2ND EDITION

A True Story

BY

DAVE ROHEE

ISBN-13:
978-1-951742-97-3 [Paperback Edition]
978-1-951742-96-6 [eBook Edition]

Printed and bound in The United States of America.

Email: *daverohee@gmail.com*
Tel: 561 818-4450

Published by

The Mulberry Books, LLC.
8330 E Quincy Avenue,
Denver CO 80237

themulberrybooks.ctom

To – Katy
Who has given me so much more than love!
And the time and space to complete
this important project

PREFACE

This is a story that had to be written. It is the true story of international kidnapping. It has taken the better part of 10 years for me to get over the horror, the nightmares, and the dangerous situation I was in. Mainly due in no small part to my lack of knowledge of China and the depths of deceit and cunning of many of the supposed entrepreneurs trying to make China a better place.

Unfortunately, I was initially an unwitting participant in a sordid tale of corruption at some of the higher levels of agencies in the Chinese administration. I was not familiar with the customs and business practices in this country and was led like the proverbial lamb to slaughter.

Once I discovered to my dismay that I was misled, I tried to disengage myself from the very forces that promised to assist me in achieving my goals. This was to no avail, and I found myself at the end of a long journey with nothing to show but a crushed ego, a failed business and, a financial disaster.

There was however, a silver lining in all this misery. There were probably hundreds of people in many law enforcement agencies in China, Canada and Interpol as well as the Canadian Embassy in Beijing and the Canadian Consulate in Shanghai, who had a hand in helping to bring me home safely. This is the amazing story.

To the RCMP, Detectives and Police officials in Coquitlam, British Columbia, Canada, my everlasting appreciation for helping to keep my spouse safe from harm. She helped save my life, probably thanks to her emergency aviation training, her knowledge of Chinese culture and, the support of law enforcement.

To the many that I cannot acknowledge for obvious reasons, you know who you were, and you have my undying gratitude for all the invaluable help and assistance you gave me, before during and after that terrifying event. I will always remember you.

Forever Grateful,

Dave Rohee

Table of Contents

CHAPTER 1

We were driving along a narrow tree-lined street in a dimly lit area when suddenly the car swerved onto the side of the road and came to a sudden stop. Both back doors opened. Two heavy-set men jumped in, pinned my legs together and jammed their elbows on top of my thighs. Someone slammed my head into the front seat headrest! Kidnapped! You hear the word, and never give it a thought that it might apply to you.

The two people in the front seat did not utter a word while this was happening. I knew this was a set-up and felt as stupid as a schoolboy in a new school with no friendly faces and no idea of what to do next!

Suddenly all sorts of thoughts and fears ran through my brain. I had no idea what was happening to me, other than I had no freedom of movement and was in fear for my life. Here I was a stranger in a foreign country, unable to speak the language and totally frightened out of my mind.

As I struggled to sit up, I was brutally hit on the back of my head which stunned me for a few seconds. I was unable to think clearly. No one said anything for a few minutes as the car raced along. A couple of minutes later the car swerved again to the side of the road. With my head just at the level of the window, out of the corner of my eye, I saw another vehicle in an open space flash its lights. The car pulled back onto the road and, the two men pulled a heavy dirty and foul-smelling bag over my head. By this time, I was crazy with fear and thoughts of my life ending sometime soon. I had no idea why this was happening or the reason for the kidnapping. I cursed myself for trying to start a new aviation operation in this godforsaken country.

We kept driving for what seemed like hours. Since I could not see my watch, I had no idea how far we had traveled or where we were headed. All I know is I was paralyzed with all sorts of thoughts about what would happen to me. No one knew where I am or who kidnapped me.

It is Sunday afternoon in Beijing, and I was not expected to show up at my office until Monday morning. And since I was the boss, nobody would give a thought to where I was or be concerned until much later in the day. My office staff was very efficient and had lots of work to keep them busy.

After what seemed like an eternity, the car finally came to a stop. I was dragged out of the car with the bag still over my head. The two guys on each side of me were literally manhandling me up a few steps and into some type of dwelling. I was roughly shoved onto a bed and, the bag removed from my head.

After I regained my eyesight, I saw my captors for the first time. This confused me even more as I did not recognize anyone and, no one spoke English! There were three men, all Chinese, and very scary looking.

One man who seemed to be in charge and giving what I assumed were instructions to the other two. One was a chubby younger man with a round typical Asian face. He had gaps between his front teeth and smiled like you were the next thing on his menu.

The third man was a very hard looking individual with partially hidden tattoos on his upper arms, a 5.00 o'clock shadow, pockmarked skin and, short spikey hair. I felt an immediate fear of this guy. He smelled as if he had not bathed in a week, dressed very shabbily in a stained khaki shirt and trousers that looked two sizes large for him.

I immediately began to perspire and felt short of breath, my heart beating a thousand beats a minute and sure to quit very soon. Dying was definitely a sure-fire conclusion and, I badly needed to pee. I looked around at my surroundings and realized that I was in serious trouble. The place was dirty, smelled like it hadn't been cleaned in years and, probably used as some type of detention cell.

There were all kinds of filthy debris on the ground, a grungy bathroom with no door and cobwebs everywhere! I was in what appeared to be a one-bedroom apartment with a broken-down bed, a small side table and, nothing else. There was a dirty flowered curtain covering a wall at one end that may have been a window. There was one door leading to what I assumed was another room or a hallway to the outside.

We waited for some time, which seemed like hours. I was feeling the weight of the world on my lungs and tried to breathe normally. Suddenly the outside door opened and someone came into the room. Imagine my relief at recognizing this new arrival! I started screaming at him, "Why have you done this?", and immediately one of the other men slapped me hard on the side of the head.

I was told to shut up by the young chubby man who was the driver of the car, and I was astonished at his ability to speak English. He seemed to be the only English spoke thug of the three men in the car during the kidnapping. The woman had never said another word during the ride. I never saw her again.

The new arrival who I knew as Albert gave me an evil smile.

"I told you this was my country, and I am going to get you thrown out." He said.

"I will have your visa revoked, take away your business and, send you back to Canada. I warned you that I had introduced you to the Chinese University last year where you made a deal to sell aviation courses and I wanted a share of your business. You refused to agree with me to be your partner, and now I am going to take everything you have".

I was speechless at this point. "I never agreed for you to become my partner," I said.

"You misrepresented yourself and your capabilities. All I have managed to do since I came to China two years ago is pay *guanxi* (Chinese slang for a bribe) to you and your connections, and nothing has ever materialized for my business to become certified".

"I have had to do this on my own and have paid thousands of US dollars to lawyers to get my aviation business licensed and certified in this country, no thanks to you," I was really pissed off.

"You also told me that you had a great location for an office. I followed your advice which, turned out to be bogus. After waiting for our official business license, we were told that it would not be approved as the location was not suitable for a foreign business!"

"What a crock of garbage your advice turned out to be. We had to break the lease and move to a new location in one of the business locations our lawyer finally was able to get approved."

"You really led me down the garden path and royally screwed me. All you have done is cost me money." I said, disgustedly.

Well, he said, "I saw the press release from the Canadian Embassy that you signed a deal with the Civil Aviation University in Tianjin to offer pilot training. I intend to make sure that I am going to run that business".

"I said, "That will only happen over my dead body."

Albert said, "That can be arranged. Don't push me."

He picked up the small pouch I usually walk with that had all my papers, a translation unit for Chinese phrases, my wallet, and an electronic database where I kept my contacts. He picked up the database unit and turned it on. He began scrolling through the contacts and said, "Who is Winnie Rohee?"

"That's my mother."

Well, he said, "Maybe she would be willing to pay your ransom to get you back alive."

I retorted, "You might as well kill me now. If you even think about calling my mother, that will be the end of her life. She is almost blind and living in an assisted facility and has no money to ransom me."

He kept scrolling and came across my son's name. "What about Chris? Do you think he might care what happened to his old man if the ransom isn't paid?"

I was so upset, and I have this sinking feeling inside that I could not even reply.

Albert said, "Do you think anyone wants you back alive? Maybe nobody gives a shit what happens to you!"

"Now, I have you where I want you. I'm going to get all your money, then have your visa revoked, and get you out of my country."

"Remember all those guys I introduced you to at the Kempinski Hotel when you arrived? Well they were good friends of mine and, all are connected to the PLA" (People's Liberation Army). They know all the ways to get you out of China".

Albert said, "Actually, we already have someone to talk to about paying the ransom, and pretty sure they have the money."

The real question is, "Are they willing to part with the money for your ransom?"

At this point, I was close to pissing in my pants. I felt that this was not going to end well.

Then he said, "I know where your wife is! She is in Shanghai on a layover and, we were having her watched."

I was dumbfounded as I now realized that this was a well-planned operation and, I was the most gullible asshole alive! Thoughts began to rush through my head. I began to realize that I had been set up since last week and fell for it, hook, line, and sinker!

My wife, Teresita, was a senior flight attendant for Air Canada and was indeed on a layover in Shanghai! I was now in turmoil as to how this was going to end. Thoughts began to run through my mind over how this could have happened and realized how naïve I was in believing that I could come to this vast country, not speaking the language, and trying to start a business.

What a foolish venture that will probably end up with me in some forgotten grave in China. She in fact, had said to me when I was developing the plan to start a flight school. "Do you really think that the Chinese will allow you to start this training program?" These people have been doing business longer than any other part of the world and will steal you blind." What prophetic words these turned out to be!

Suddenly other thoughts began running through my head. The difficulties I had when I arrived in this very closed society and a really backward situation regarding aviation and flight training and a host of other issues I had to deal with over the past two years. All came flooding into my head. I began to feel that the future was indeed dim and looking dimmer by the minute.

Albert broke into my thoughts when he said, "I know Teresita is in Shanghai. We were going to call her and tell her that the ransom is Five Hundred Thousand US Dollars and has to be paid by this weekend."

At this point, I started to figure out that I had to get a message to her somehow without alerting the kidnappers. Not sure how I was going to handle this, and feeling I had to try at least, I made up my mind to go for it if I got a chance to speak to her.

Next thing I knew, Albert gets on the phone and talks to someone in Cantonese. Obviously, not knowing what he said was very worrisome, and my concern was for Teresita's safety. After a couple of minutes, he is off the phone and then turned to me.

He said, "She is in her hotel room. I'm warning you again, don't say a word about where you are (I had absolutely no clue) and who we were." I realized that she was being watched.

Then he called the Hotel where Air Canada puts up their crews and asked for her room. Then just as the phone is answered, Albert without saying a word, handed the phone to the guy who seemed to be in charge of the others, and said talk. The guy had a type of military bearing, well dressed and had a green fabric watch band with an unusual watch face on his wrist. I made a mental note that I was going to remember these guys if I lived and decided to call him the 'Major.'

The 'Major' started talking very fast in Cantonese for a few minutes and then listened for what seemed like an eternity, which was probably no more than five minutes. Then he handed the phone back to Albert who covered the phone with his hand and said to me.

"Okay, you remember what I said to you. Only tell her exactly what I told you and no more."

When he handed me the phone, I was speechless for a few seconds until I heard Teresita's voice! Then I started to babble and crying at the same time. Not even sure what I said until I felt a hard slap on the back of my head. I calmed down and said, "I have been kidnapped, and they want Five Hundred Thousand Dollars for my release."

She started crying and said, "Who did this to you?"

At that point, I remembered that there is no way for her to pay any kind of ransom and felt that this was it for me.

I shouted, "They are going to kill me if they don't get the money by Saturday."

Albert grabbed the phone away from me and gave it back to the Major. The Major talked again for a few minutes and then disconnected the call.

After the call, Albert said the Major had told Teresita that she could get the money from her brother, who owned seven well-established restaurants in Vancouver, British Columbia, where we lived. He did not tell me what Teresita had said to the Major.

What happened next surprised me. Albert opened the back of the phone and removed the SIM card. This would become an important aspect of the kidnapping that I was not aware of at the time. Albert then left the room after issuing what sounded like instructions to the three men.

During the kidnapping process, I had feigned a heart problem when they put the bag over my face, but it apparently did not concern anyone at the time.

Just before Albert left the room, I said, "I have a heart condition and if I don't get my medication, you will probably not be able to collect ransom on a dead person."

That stopped him for a few minutes. He walked around the small room, talking to someone on the phone.

He then said, "Are you taking medication?"

"Yes, every day." I said to him.

He said, "Where is the medication?" I said it was in my apartment in a small overnight bag I usually traveled with. At this point, I was hoping that this would alert someone as to why I was missing and perhaps the authorities would get involved. I was not sure he would have been able to get into my apartment as everyone coming to see me had to announce who they were visiting. Then security would call the person, and if cleared, a slip would be written out for the resident to sign on the way out.

He did not say another word and left. It was now late Sunday night, and the only one that spoke any English was the youngest guy who I called Baby Face. He had a round face with black beady eyes, long black hair, and smooth skin. He was very talkative, both in English and Cantonese. While I only learned the basic language skills in Mandarin, I was not able to follow any of the dialogue between the three kidnappers.

There was only one double bed in the room with a dingy, dirty, smelly mattress, and a stained sheet. I was told by Baby Face that he and I were sleeping on the bed. He made me take off my shoes and get on the bed, which was next to a wall. He wanted me to sleep on the inside next to the wall. I took off my shoes and got on the bed. He made me lie down on my back.

Baby Face then took a heavy long winter parka that was hanging from a nail behind the door and made me put my left arm through one of the sleeves. The coat was rancid and smelled like old shoes and smelly feet! He then got on the bed and put his right arm through the second sleeve and then zipped up the coat. We were now effectively joined together, which felt very weird. I found that I could not move in any direction without him knowing. There was no way to turn on my side, so I felt very trapped and paranoid at this point only a few hours after the kidnapping.

There was a lot of talk during this time between the Major and the hard-looking dude number three. I was so afraid of this guy I did not even name him at the time. He was just number three and an evil-looking man. Anyway, the Major then looked around the room and went to the far wall that was covered by a cloth curtain. He swept it aside, and from the bed, I could see that there were two windows and one door. Both the windows and the door had metal bars like a jail cell would have, and obviously, this place looked and felt like a jail.

Once the Major checked the door to make sure it was secure, he let the curtain down and talked to number three. The Major then left the room and came back in with a sleeping bag. When the Major left, Number three closed and locked the door and put the key in his pocket. He then placed the sleeping bag on the floor right next to the door and zipped himself in. He looked like he is in place for the night. I decided that he should be called 'Ugly man.'

Right then, I was having all sorts of desperate thoughts about trying to escape from this place. It seemed that all the exits and possible escape route via the back door, were out of consideration. I was now out of options and worried shitless. I tried to relax, but sleep did not come for a long time. I couldn't even toss or turn and tied to the jerk next to me I felt like crap. How was this going to end, I wondered?

Chapter 2

Teresita
Shanghai, Sunday night

When the phone rang, I was surprised as the rest of the crew had gone out for dinner and I was not expecting any calls. When I picked up the phone a voice in heavy Cantonese said. "Is this Teresita Li?"

I said "Yes, who is this?"

"Never mind," he replied, "We have your husband and we want a ransom for his release."

"What? You must be joking, who IS this?"

"No joke," he said. "We kidnapped him tonight, and we want five hundred thousand US dollars for his release. His name is Dave Rohee, and you must deliver the money by Saturday in Beijing."

"I don't believe you! And why would you kidnap him? He doesn't have that kind of money! Why didn't you kidnap someone who has money?"

He then said, "Shut up, woman and listen."

So, I listened, and what I heard was hard to believe. He said that they knew my brother had lots of restaurants back in Vancouver and that he was a millionaire. He said I must ask my brother to pay the money to get Dave released. He also told me that I was being watched, and not to leave the hotel at any time until the return flight to Vancouver which was scheduled to depart late Monday.

At this time, I was really worried and not sure what to do. Then I remembered that Dave had met with a Canadian Consul official for Shanghai. He and one of Dave's friends from DeHavilland went out a few times for dinner and drinks in Beijing and Shanghai. I had Daryl's number in my cell phone and called him immediately.

When he picked up, I said, "Daryl, this is Teresita, Dave's wife. We met at your home last year."

"Hi, Teresita, I remember. Is Dave still in Beijing? I know he was trying to get a flying school started in China and figured that he would be the only one to try something that difficult in this country."

"Your guy does not know the meaning of the words – can't be done! China has to be the hardest place to try and start a new business for any foreigner. I have been here for three years for DeHavilland Aircraft as a Tech Rep and have barely gotten started with what I came to do for the company. This place will drive you nuts. Everything must go through multiple agents and corrupt officials just looking for a bribe. They will delay you every step of the way and then try to steal your business." Daryl said.

"Daryl, this is a bad time for me. I just got a call from some guy who said they had kidnapped him and wanted me to pay a ridiculous ransom for him."

"I remembered you introduced us to one of the Canadian Consulate officials here in Shanghai and wondered if he would be able to help me. I don't know what else to do. I am on a layover flight and due to depart Pudong International airport at 6.30 tomorrow night for Vancouver."

"Oh, my God! Tell you what Teresita, why don't you come over here and we can talk to Allan when you get here. He knows where I live, and he can see if there is something he can do. Since Dave is a Canadian citizen, I'm sure there are procedures for this type of problem."

I started crying and managed to choke back the tears and said, "They told me not to leave the hotel as I was being watched. I really need some help."

"Are you sure they are watching you?" Daryl said.

"I don't want to take a chance and have something horrible happen to Dave or me," I said.

"Ok, Teresita, calm down. I understand. I will call Allan and see what he says and call you right back." Daryl tells me.

I put down the phone, laid down on the bed, and cried. I knew this was not a good idea to try and start a business in China, and now we are both in trouble. I don't think my brother will agree to pay any ransom for Dave. He never really liked him that much and always felt that I should have had a relationship with someone we knew in our circle of friends. I kept worrying about this and felt that we had had a great relationship over the past 12 years. We were common-law spouses who are legal in Canada, but my family had not always agreed with this. My sister had pushed us to get married several times, but we both agreed that it was not necessary. We both had previous marriages that did not work out that well.

After about 20 minutes, the hotel phone rang. "Hello Teresita, this is Allan. I heard from Daryl that Dave has been kidnapped in Beijing. I can't believe this has happened."

"Hello Allan, thank you for calling. I am afraid and don't know what to do or where to turn. I need some help and wonder if you could tell me what I should be doing."

"Okay, Teresita, first give me your cell number. Do not make any more calls through the hotel switchboard as many of the hotels that cater to foreigners in China have agreements with the PLA to bug hotel rooms, and telephone conversations are never as private as you would expect."

"The **P**eople's **L**iberation **A**rmy has all kinds of power and in fact, have 'cart blanche' to do whatever is necessary to keep foreigners in line, so be very careful who you speak to about this problem."

I started crying again and asked him, "What should I do? I have to leave China tomorrow night but don't know what to do now."

"Here is what is going to happen. I am coming over to your hotel, and we can discuss this in private. I have a lot of connections that can possibly help, but I need the full picture of what was said, and then I will decide where we go from here."

My first thought, however, is that you need to head back home as scheduled on your regular flight. At least you will be safe at home in Vancouver, and I only have to focus on Dave's situation." Allan said to me.

"Oh Allan, thank you, thank you so much. How soon can you get here?" I said.

"I will be there in half-an-hour. Do NOT open your door for anybody else. I will call you on your cell when I get to your floor, so you will know it's me. I have your room number from Daryl, so no one will know I am coming to meet you. I know that hotel very well as I regularly meet up with some of Air Canada's pilots who I know."

After I gave him my cell number and hung up, I collapsed back on the bed. I felt hot tears falling onto the pillow and wanted to make the problem go away. Then after a few minutes, I calmed down to where I began to feel that Allan was going to help, and perhaps he could turn this miserable situation into a successful conclusion.

I then began to think about who would do something like this. Is it somebody we knew? Could it be some people Dave met when he came here two years ago? So many questions and no real answers.

Chapter 3

Teresita
Shanghai, Later Sunday night

My cell phone rang! I jumped up from the bed and grabbed the phone off the table next to the bed.

"Hello, Allan?"

"Yes, Teresita, it's me. I am almost at your door. Wait for my knock. Don't open until you hear me."

I heard a light knock on the door. I looked through the peephole and saw a floppy rain hat covering most of a face that I really could not see very well, but having had the phone call, I knew it was Allan.

I opened the door and literally grabbed him and hugged him. He patted me on the back and said, "Okay, Teresita, let's close the door, and then we can talk." Allan came in, locked the door and made sure the security latch was engaged.

The room was pretty small, so Allan took the one chair in the room, and I sat on the bed. I had tissues all balled up scattered all over the bed and almost started crying again. But just having him there made me feel much better.

"Start at the beginning and tell me what happened," Allan said.

I related everything that happened from the time I came back to my room after dinner and the phone rang. Allan was very quiet and calmly asked lots of questions about what I heard from the kidnappers. He also asked if I might know who had kidnapped him and why.

"Do you have any idea who might be behind this type of thing." He said.

"China has a long history of kidnappings, killings, maiming's, etc. but never of a foreigner and especially Canadians. We are really liked in China. So why Dave?"

"And there never has been a kidnapping of a Canadian in China, so this is a first."

I said. "Is there anything you can do?"

"Yes, there is!" Allan says.

"First, I am going to alert the Embassy in Beijing tonight and get the ball rolling for them to contact the Chinese authorities to alert them that a Canadian had been kidnapped in Beijing, and any assistance they could give us would be greatly appreciated. We have an excellent relationship with the Chinese government and the present administration, including some higher-ups in the intelligence services.

Allan also said, "I'm sure by this time tomorrow the Chinese Secret Police will be fully informed, and helping to try and identify, and locate the kidnappers. They do not want to have this type of negative publicity on the eve of a very high-profile political summit of the Chinese leadership in Beijing."

"It starts in two weeks, and this would really be a black eye for the Chinese leaders to have to face the media."

"Wow. Allan. Thank you so much."

"Not a problem Teresita. Now here is what I need you to do. I need you to take your normal routine flight back to Canada, so at least I have one less person to worry about. I imagine that you have to report this to Air Canada."

"Of course, I have to tell them. And I'm not sure what they will want to do. This a crazy mess and I can't even begin to understand this situation." I started crying again, and now my eyes were all red and swollen. I must look a real sight. I grab some more tissues and try to wipe my eyes. Now at least I have some help.

"Is there someone who worked the flight whom you know that can stay with you tonight? I don't want you to be alone tonight."

"Well, the first person I have to call is the Purser. She is the lead flight attendant and responsible for the flight crew, other than the pilots, and she has to be notified as soon as one of us has a problem, like getting sick, food poisoning, etc. Not sure if any of them have ever dealt with something like this."

Allan said, "Why don't you call her now before I leave, so at least I have an indication of what procedures she will be following."

"I know some of the crew went out for dinner and pretty sure she went with them. They don't usually come back to the hotel until late. Our flight doesn't leave until tomorrow evening, so they can afford to stay out late. Let me try her room."

"Okay, but don't tell her why you're calling."

I look up our room assignment list and try Cheryl's number. No answer. I leave a message asking her to call me when she gets back.

Allan stays for a while, but by 10.30, he says he needs to get the ball rolling and wants to use the secure phone system at the Consul

General's office. He gives me a long hug and tries to calm me as I started crying again.

"Try not to get too worked up Teresita, you need to be strong, and we will get through this together."

When Allan leaves, I make sure the door is locked, and the security latch is engaged.

I get ready for bed. Sleep does not come easily. I am hoping that the phone will ring, and someone will tell me this was just a bad joke! No such luck. And I don't hear from Cheryl either. I tossed and turned all night. I woke up crying with my nose running. I have used up two boxes of tissues that were provided by the hotel and now using a face towel to dry my eyes.

I kept asking myself why Dave had to put himself in a situation where he didn't speak the language, and yet here he is trying to start a flying school in China of all places. Our family left China and Hong Kong just because of the many social injustices that plagued this country for centuries. And here I am trying to help him extricate himself from this disaster. I only hoped he could be rescued in one piece and not injured. This was not a great place to be a foreigner.

Chapter 4

Teresita
Shanghai, Monday

Cheryl calls me at 8.30 am.

"What's up, Teresita? You have a bad night?" We missed you at dinner. We always need you for translation duty, but we were able to get through the night, ok."

"Cheryl, you have no idea just how bad. Anyway, could you come to my room as soon as possible?"

"Alright, girl, give me a few minutes to look decent, and I'll be right over."

A knock on the door. I looked through the peephole and saw Cheryl.

I opened the door and began crying in her arms. She put her arms around me, and we stagger over to the bed. Once we sat down, I finally settled down and began to tell her what happened.

"You know whenever we fly into Beijing I always take a few days off to spend with Dave since he is now living here full time. You are not going to believe this. He got kidnapped yesterday!"

"My God, Teresita, tell me this is a joke," Cheryl said.

"No joke, deadly serious and very worrying. I need you to tell me what the procedures are for something like this?"

"Teresita, I have been with the airline seventeen years and never heard of anything like this. And even more shocking that it has happened to someone I know. I know Dave has been to quite a few Air Canada parties, retirement bashes, and knows some of our pilots. He usually sits in the cockpit whenever he flies into Beijing. I have seen him on a few flights that I worked into Beijing."

I tell Cheryl what I know to this point, including the fact that a Canadian Consul official for Shanghai is a friend of Dave's, and he was here with me last night. She agrees that this is probably a good idea that the Consul's office in Shanghai is involved, and no doubt, the Embassy in Beijing will be involved as well.

She told me that she had to call the Captain as he was responsible for the entire crew's safety in the air and on any layovers. She called Derek, and he agreed to come over right after breakfast. He arrived at around 10.20 am. He had a hard time believing that Dave had been kidnapped in Beijing and being held for ransom. He said he knows Dave by sight and seen him on a few Vancouver – Beijing flights. We told him the rest of the story, including the fact that the Canadian authorities have been alerted and were going to help.

Derek said that he needed to notify the airline immediately. I told him about the PLA bugging phones and not to use the hotel switchboard to make any calls regarding Dave's situation. He agreed and said he would take a cab to the Air Canada operations office at the airport and send a secure message to the company by our internal messaging system. He said they have to be notified immediately, and he would wait for instructions before heading back to the hotel. He left us to head to the airport.

Cheryl stays with me for another few hours, and I was able to feel more like myself. She has been a big help just by staying with me while I got my wits together.

In the early afternoon, just after we have a room service lunch, Derek returned and let us know that the airline had told him how we deal with the situation at our end. The flight would return to Vancouver as scheduled. The rest of the crew were not to be notified so that the flight could be handled normally, and the passengers would not feel uncomfortable for the eleven-hour plus flight.

The company had recommended that I not work during the flight. I told Derek and Cheryl, "It would be better for me to have something to do rather than just sit around worrying, and the rest of the crew would keep asking, *'what's up with Teresita.'* Since I am working the first-class galley, I will be mostly on my own, and near to the cockpit in case I need a break, or just to talk to you. Keeping busy with running the galley will at least help to keep my mind off the problem."

They both agreed that this would more than likely be the better of the two options. So, we parted company, and I began to prepare for my departure.

My heart is still hurting, and I am quite scared. However, now that Allan and the Embassy, Cheryl, Derek, and the company had been informed, I was not feeling so alone. My face was a mess from all the crying, and major makeup was required to make me look presentable.

At crew pick-up at the hotel, I made sure that I am the last to arrive, so I won't have to sit and wait for the airline transport and have to talk to anyone. Cheryl also got right next to me and sat with me in the van. We held hands but didn't talk at all. She looked at me with a sad expression. I can feel her concern, which I really appreciated.

Air Canada Flight, Shanghai – Vancouver
Monday evening, Prior to Boarding

We went through the sign-in processss with little hold-up, and I managed to keep my head down and busy in the galley and made sure that all the equipment, ovens, micros, and food items were all correct and accounted for the long flight back home. Derek came out of the cockpit and gave me a quick hug.

"Teresita, everything will work out okay! Are you sure you will be okay working the flight?"

"Yes, Derek, I am feeling a lot better, but almost wish I could be in Beijing while this is happening."

"I feel sure that the Embassy, RCMP and Chinese authorities are doing everything possible to have a safe outcome to this problem. Try to stay calm and not worry too much."

The flight takes off as scheduled, and I feel some relief that I am now on my way home. I am worrying all the time about how Dave is holding up. This is a real problem, and I frequently go into the restroom in the galley and have a cry for a few minutes. No one else had realized what I was experiencing was a good thing. I didn't want to have to discuss the kidnapping.

When I got my crew rest period, I couldn't relax or doze off as I normally did, so finally, I gave up and head to the cockpit for a few minutes. The Captain turned around in his seat, saw me, and smiled.

"Hey, Teresita, how are you feeling?"

"Not too bad considering," I replied.

Derek said. "Why don't you head back to the galley. I will come and talk to you."

I headed back into the first-class galley and told Donna that she could take her break early.

Donna asked, "Everything ok?"

I managed to convince her that I couldn't sleep and wanted to keep busy. She was glad for the early rest period and headed to the rest area where we have a small narrow bunk. It is a quiet area in the Boeing 767 that both the pilots and flight attendants take their breaks on the long overseas flights.

I waited anxiously for Derek to come out of the cockpit. After another 12 minutes of looking at the clock on the microwave oven in the galley, the cockpit door opened, and Derek entered the galley. He opened the curtain into the first-class cabin and looked to see if anyone was nearby. After he closed the curtain, he said. "Teresita, I have notified Flight Operations of your situation, and here is what I know at this point."

"On arrival in Vancouver, you will be the first to deplane, and before any passengers. You will be met by the Base Manager and escorted to the exit door leading down to the ramp. You will be met by two RCMP officers who will escort you through customs and out of the terminal. Make sure you take all your flight bags and personal items with you. The RCMP will be taking you home. They are concerned about your safety, so they're not taking any chances."

Teresita says. "Oh, Derek, this is crazy! What am I supposed to do? I can barely keep my emotions in check. I feel like I'm losing it."

"I know how this looks, Teresita, but you need to try to keep calm and let the authorities handle it. I'm sure you will be ok, and I can only hope that Dave will be released safely. Are you able to finish the flight in the galley, or would you like to be relieved of that extra workload?"

"I feel it would be better to keep busy. Maybe it will help not to have to think about it too much. Thanks, Derek, really appreciate your help. Please don't say anything else to the other crew members. I have not told anyone else other than Cheryl."

"No problem at all. I don't want the other crew members knowing too much at this stage, either. The less said, the better. Only the copilot and Cheryl know, and I want to keep it that way." Derek says.

Derek heads back into the cockpit, and I tried to stay calm. There were almost two hours left in the flight, and I began to prepare for the breakfast service. This was the last service on this long flight. The other first-class and business class flight attendants were assembling the trolleys for the service. This activity keeps me occupied and busy for the next 45 minutes.

The galley was very busy at this time, so no one seemed to notice that I was quieter than usual and not my normal happy self. Fortunately, there were no unhappy passengers during this breakfast service, and I was grateful for this lull prior to whatever would face me on arrival in Vancouver.

As we started our descent into the Vancouver (YVR) airport, I made sure all the trolleys were locked in place, all loose items were stowed, and doors secured. This usually would take me 15 to 20 minutes, and this day I was constantly checking everything two or three times just to make sure I had not missed or forgotten anything critical for safety on landing. The captain made the pre-landing announcement, and after my last check, all the flight attendants take their seats and buckle in.

Now I started to worry about the whole kidnapping disaster all over again. All kinds of thoughts were running rampant through my mind, and Cindy, who is very perceptive and a cute gal who works with me on several long flights, asks me. "Teresita, are you ok? You are very quiet and not your usual bubbly self."

"I managed to tell her that I was not feeling too great and must be coming down with something. She said they all missed me at dinner and hoped I would be all right."

Just then, the intercom chimed, and I picked up the phone on the wall right behind me. Derek said. "Teresita, are you all set."

"I replied, yes. Thanks for your help, Derek."

As soon as we landed and began taxiing to the terminal, I unbuckled my four-way restraint and got up to get my bags.

Cindy says. "Teresita, what's going on?"

"They want me to leave first in case I have a bug that should be checked out before we let any passengers off at the gangway." She did not say anything but gave me a look that I couldn't define.

Just then, Cheryl arrived at the front of the aircraft and gave me a big hug. "Everything will be okay, Teresita. Try not to worry about it. There is nothing you can do. Let the folks who deal with this stuff, handle it."

I tried to answer her, but my eyes tear up, and I could barely make out her face. Somehow, I managed to thank her. Cindy gave me another look, and I felt she knows that this is more than a bug or not feeling well. I tried not to look at her as we positioned to open the main cabin door.

Chapter 5

Kidnapped Location
Somewhere south of Beijing, Monday

I felt a rustling next to me and the awareness that something was not right. All of a sudden, the realization that I must be in the middle of a nightmare hits me. And then it dawned on me that it was not a nightmare, it was actually real! The sleeve my left arm was in, got pulled and I realized that Baby Face, the kidnapper just gotten up and was trying to unzip the jacket. Not sure how long I slept, but at some point, I had managed to sleep in spite of the uncomfortable position I was forced to endure, and the rank smell of the parka and the stained bed-sheet.

His face was only a few inches away from me, and his breath smelled like a sewer. He smiled and said. "You okay?" I tried not to gasp from the smell but managed to nod my head. He unzipped the parka all the way, and we separated from each other.

I did not know what time it was. They took away my watch and wallet when we got to this place last night. I now need to take a piss and try to get cleaned up. I told Baby Face I needed to pee. He let me get off the bed, and I noticed then that the bedroom door was now open, and the Ugly guy was not there. The sleeping bag was folded up next to the door. I now realized with horror that this place had a sinister purpose! I imagined others being kept here for a similar purpose. It must have been used as a prison. I wondered how many others might have suffered from this scenario?

Baby Face allowed me to go into the toilet and do my business. No privacy, no door. When I turned on the water in the filthy sink, a dribble of brown water started, and I decided that I was not going to try and use that to rinse my mouth. I had no toothbrush or toothpaste even if I were to take a gamble the water would probably have done some serious damage to my health.

When I came out of the narrow toilet, I noticed that there was no shower or place to have a shower. I realized that I really was in some backwoods location. I was now very worried about my prospects of leaving this place alive.

Baby Face made me go back into the bedroom, and when I tried looking back, I saw another small area that I guess was a living room of some sort, very small and cramped. I could not see anything else, and he made me get back on the bed. I sat there, dirty, miserable, and looked around. The curtain was now brightly lit from the sun, and I could see how dingy and horrible this place really was.

A short time later, the Ugly guy reappeared with a couple of plastic bags. The bags held a few different items, hard bread, some type of baked rolls and bananas. There were a few bottles of water as well. He made a gesture that said I could have what I wanted. I took a banana, a bottle of water and one of the rolls. My mouth felt as if some animal had crawled up in there and died, and my teeth felt furry and disgusting.

After I had what passed for my breakfast, I lay back down on the bed. The two kidnappers began talking away and perhaps arguing among themselves. I had no idea what was going on but worried about Teresita was.

Then I thought about what brought me to China and the concept of starting a flight school in this backward country. I must have been delusional to think that I could manage to actually get a flight school certified. I have never been one to shy away from a challenge, and this was a major one for sure.

I remembered all the various meetings that Albert had arranged with the Chinese Aviation Authority (CAAC) to get my plan accepted. Every meeting was preceded by a payment called 'guanxi' (otherwise known as a bribe). Nothing, however, came out of any of these meetings, except lunches and dinners at exotic restaurants and copious amounts of *Baijo*. The clear toxic concoction that is the strongest and most potent alcohol I had ever tasted. When you have a business meeting at a restaurant in China, toasts were the order of the day. Many toasts every few minutes. Lots of *Baijo*. And consequently, many tipsy diners. Usually, ten diners to a table with the guest of honor sitting next to the head of the table.

Not being much of a drinker, I tried to avoid the *Baijo* as much as possible. Olivia, my office manager, and also my translator would be sitting right next to me and substituting her water glass for my *Baijo* and then emptying the glass with *Baijo* under the table. We became quite good at this sleight of hand, and this was my only way of saving grace to be able to function with a clear head for the duration of the meeting.

The time passed slowly, and the thought that I had been taken for a real ride became evident in my thinking process and how gullible I was.

Sometime later in the morning, the Major arrived and began talking to the other two kidnappers for some time. Shortly after this,

Albert arrived and threw a small overnight bag at me. Then he said, "Make sure you have your medication. Let me know if it's all there."

I opened the bag and looked through the various items I took on my regular trips to Hong Kong. My medication was there as well as a small black bag with toothbrush, toothpaste, deodorant, and a few other items we tended to collect over the years. There was also a paperback that I had purchased in HK on my last trip and had not read as yet. I could not believe my eyes what I read the title. It was "Hostage" by Robert Crais! This was unreal. Not sure how this one ends, but sure hope it turns out to be a good result for the hostage. I told him the medication was all there. He didn't respond.

Then suddenly a cell phone rings. Baby Face reached into his pocket and took out his phone and answered it. He listened for a couple of minutes and then began yelling in Cantonese to whoever is on the phone with him. After a few minutes of this, he shut off the phone. The others all talked to him at the same time. They shout at him for a few minutes. He eventually calmed down and probably told them what they wanted to know. This phone call would become very important later in the week.

Alberts said something to the Major, and they both had a lengthy discussion. Shortly thereafter, Albert took out his cell phone and removed the SIM card. He then inserted another SIM card and made a call. When the phone call connected, he handed the phone to the Major.

The Major spoke very quickly, and whoever picked up the phone obviously knew the language. He looked at me a few times during the call and I realized that he must be talking to Teresita. He looked at Albert and said something.

Albert turned to me and said. "Ok Dave, talk to Teresita and let her know you are fine. Don't say anything else. Baby Face went into the other room and came back with the dirty kitchen knife. He stuck the point in my ear, but did not make contact with my skin and said, "Say the right thing now."

I felt hope surging through my body, and some excitement bubbled up from somewhere. I grabbed the cell phone. "Teresita? Is that you?"

"Yes, it's me. What have they done to you? Are you ok?"

"Up to now, I'm ok. The kidnappers tell me that if you can't deliver the money by Saturday, that will be the end of it."

"What do you mean the end of it?" She asked.

"I think that if you can't find someone to pay the five hundred thousand dollars that they will kill me!" Albert grabbed the phone back and handed it to the Major. He said a few more words, then ended the call.

Chapter 6

Teresita
Vancouver, Monday
Vancouver, 12 hours behind Beijing

The gangway bumped gently against the side of the aircraft. I undid the safety panel, turned the big handle, and unlocked the main exit door. As soon as the door opened, I noticed the base manager standing there. He looked at me and said.

"Do you have all your bags?"

"I have them here," I replied.

"Okay, come with me, please."

I picked up my rollaway and hanging bag and followed him onto the gangway. As soon as we got to the door leading down to the ramp, he stopped and said. "You will be meeting two RCMP police officers here. They will be escorting you out of the terminal and taking you home. The airline is always concerned about the safety of its employees, so please cooperate with them." He then opened the door, and as I passed him, he said, "Good luck Teresita. I hope everything will turn out for the better."

At the bottom of the stairs, I saw two police officers waiting for me. They were very serious looking individuals in full dress uniform. They took both my rollaway and hanging bag from me.

"Hello, Ms. Li. We will be accompanying you through customs and then taking you home."

At this time, I was overwhelmed and didn't even acknowledge these remarks. The next 30 minutes seemed like hours as we passed through the terminal basement, where all the baggage was stored and moved either to the aircraft or into the terminal, eventually to find their way onto the baggage carousels. These guys obviously knew the place very well, and we entered a back entrance almost directly into a customs holding area. We waited for a few minutes until a customs officer showed up from an interior office. The RCMP officers then explained that I had an emergency and to please clear me to enter the country. This is the normal procedure for all international flights. He made no additional comment about the emergency.

He asked if there was anything to declare, and when I shook my head, he immediately gave his approval. He did ask for my passport, and after glancing at it to confirm that I was a Canadian, he said we were free to leave the airport.

The two officers asked if I had a vehicle at the airport. I always drove myself to the airport for any long flights with layovers, and I told them the car was in the employee parking lot. As they escorted me through the terminal, I saw lots of glances from passengers and other airport employees, and I wondered what they must be thinking.

They led me to an RCMP cruiser at the curb and opened the back door for me to get in. One officer put my bags in the trunk and got into the passenger side. The other officer got into the driver's seat and asked for directions to the employee parking lot.

The Air Canada employee parking lot at YVR is adjacent to the main airline and maintenance building, which is about five minutes from the terminal and located on the approach road to YVR. When we got there and located my two-year-old Corolla, the driver pulled up behind it and said,

"Please do not get out until we have secured the area. We want to make sure the car is safe for you to drive."

They asked for the keys to the car. They both got out and approached the car cautiously and shone a flashlight into the interior. One officer opened the driver's door. The other officer opened the other doors and then walked around and opened the trunk. After making sure the car is empty, they allowed me to get out of the police cruiser.

The driver then said. "Ms. Li, we will be escorting you home. Are you ok to drive, or would you prefer to leave your car and go with us."

"I think I am okay to drive." I managed to say in a quiet voice.

"There will be two other police officers escorting you home. We will swing by the YVR police station to pick them up. They will be traveling in your car, and we will be following you home."

"I'm really grateful for all your help. Do you think all this is necessary?" I say.

"The airline has certain procedures that were in place in circumstances like these, and we are only following the rules. They are in place for your safety. They are obviously concerned that there may be international implications and want to be certain to take every precaution." The officer says.

I got in and started the car. The officers put my bags in the trunk and closed the lid. I backed up and followed the police car to the airport police station. When they stopped the cruiser, I stopped behind them. Just as we arrive, two other RCMP police officers left the station and approached the cruiser.

After talking to the officer on the passenger side, they then approached my car on the driver's side. When I opened my window, they introduced themselves as Officer Blaine and Officer Murphy. Officer Blaine told me they would ride with me to my home. I told them that I live in Coquitlam, which is almost 40 minutes from Vancouver airport.

"No problem," said Officer Blaine. We will be getting a ride back to YVR with the other cruiser as soon as we see you home safely. It's just a part of our job."

"What happens then?" I asked.

"The Coquitlam RCMP branch has already been notified by the Airline to where you live." Your home has been under surveillance since we received the first call from Air Canada."

"Once you arrive home, our places will be taken by the local RCMP officers, who will set up ongoing surveillance until this problem has been resolved. I hope you can appreciate our concerns. They will be monitoring all calls and recording any communications with the kidnappers. Obviously, we would appreciate your cooperation."

"I understand completely. I don't know who these bastards are or why they did this to Dave, but I hope they will be caught and punished for this." I said.

"Ms. Li, there are a lot of people and agencies already involved with this, so be aware that we will do whatever it takes to bring them to justice. But our priority is your husband's safe recovery and your safety!"

By this time, I was somewhat in a better frame of mind and felt very angry that this had happened to us. I know Dave might have made a bad decision to start an aviation business in China, but that should not be any reason for him to be kidnapped. I wondered if he had made any enemies while trying to get contracts with any Chinese airlines. I knew there were a lot of stories about business deals going bad in China due to large scale corruption, but kidnapping was never an issue.

Since we were 12 hours behind Beijing, and the flight time was almost 12 hours, it was still Monday in Canada. I felt the pressure starting to mount and not sure how to deal with it. I was also pretty sure that my brother would not want to even consider lending me the ransom.

He and Dave had never really bonded, and I felt it was only because he and I were legally common-law spouses that they were even civil towards each other. Dave had always felt that my brother Patrick had not treated me with the respect I deserved as his younger sister. The tradition in Chinese families is that the elder male sibling is the head of the family if the father is no longer alive. Patrick had been very successful in his life and now owned six restaurants that were doing very well.

BY this time, we were approaching Coquitlam and our home. We lived in a beautiful, gated community that was located on a hillside, overlooking the downtown area. Silver Oaks was divided into two sections, one on either side of the roadway. Our smaller enclave of the two sections overlooking Port Coquitlam was a gated area for eight homes. As we drove up the hill, I saw lots of flashing lights from two police cruisers just outside our gate. The cruiser that was following us from the airport stopped a short way down the hill, but no one got out.

Officer Blaine asked me to stop the car and let him out. He stepped out of the car and walked over to the first cruiser that was near the gate. He talked to the driver and then walked back and got into the car.

"Okay, Ms. Li. The officer said that there has been no activity since they arrived, and we can proceed."

I opened the main gate with the remote, the gate rolled back, and I turned into our driveway, which is the first one right after the gate. I then hit the remote for the garage door. Officer Blaine asked me not to get out of the car until they had inspected the home and made sure that no unauthorized person was inside.

Once inside the garage, both Officers Blaine and Murphy entered the garage door into the basement. Meantime, the two other police cruisers turned into the driveway and parked. Four officers got out and stood behind my car.

After almost 10 minutes, Officers Blaine and Murphy re-entered the garage and told me it was ok. The home had been checked and now safe for me to enter.

At this time, another unmarked black sedan arrived just outside the main gate. One of the officers asked me to open the gate as this was the detective that was in charge of the case. I opened the gate, and the sedan stopped behind the cruisers.

Three people got out of the sedan. Two men and a woman. They all approached and introduced themselves. The first Detective was in his mid-forties, I guess, and the one in charge. He told me his name was Detective George Sanders of the RCMP Coquitlam Branch. He introduced the other two as Detective Pem Avino, a younger good-looking Asian in his thirties with short dark hair and a fit and lean physique. The female was introduced as Detective Pamela Colson. A fairly well-built athletic woman, a bit taller than me with curly blonde hair. She looked like a friendly person. She smiled and shook my hand.

"We're here to help you get this safely resolved." She said.

Detective Sanders told me these would be my escorts for the duration of the negotiation with the kidnappers. He asked me to cooperate with all of them as it was in my best interest to have this matter resolved for everyone as quickly and safely as possible.

He also remarked that the international police organization Interpol had been advised that the kidnapping had taken place, and a Canadian citizen had been kidnapped in China. He told me that the Canadian Embassy in Beijing was coordinating with the Foreign Affairs Department of the Canadian government in Ottawa. The RCMP, which is responsible for the safety of Embassy staff abroad was also on high alert and aware of the kidnapped Canadian.

I felt hopeful that something would eventually happen that would avoid the need for paying any ransom, which in any case was not a possibility. I had no resources that can even remotely pay that kind of money, and Dave was always investing in new projects that took priority. He was still looking for that silver lining somewhere. I admired his positive attitude and outlook but could not see a good outcome for his aviation dreams. He had always dreamed of opening a flight school, and this was an opportunity that he could not pass up.

While I got my bags into my home, the Detectives followed me upstairs to the second level. This was where we have our master bedroom, living room, family room, and kitchen.

The third level has a large guest room with ensuite, and a small family room Dave had converted the family room into a TV, Stereo and Movie room. We spent a lot of time up there as it had a beautiful view of the high rises in downtown Coquitlam. Some mornings we sat up there and watched the low-lying fog with the tops of the buildings just poking through the tops of the mist. It was quiet and serene, and

I wondered if we would ever have the opportunity to enjoy that view again.

The Detectives had lugged up several hard side cases and asked me where they could set up their equipment. They wanted to know what would be the best location to set up the recording devices to monitor any communication with the kidnappers that was close to the landline access. Even though they first contacted me on my cell phone, the detectives felt that I should try to get them to call on the home phone. The told me the recording would be clearer on the land-line.

I told the detectives that I needed to have a shower and freshen up after my flight. Detective Colson says. "Ms. Li, please go about your normal routine, and we will adjust our schedule as necessary. Please call me Pamela."

"Well, since I'm not sure how long this will take, please call me Teresita."

Just then the home phone rang, and everyone looked startled. The Detectives have not had any time to set up their equipment, but I'm sure it could not be the kidnappers, so I pick up the phone.

"Hello. Who's calling?" I asked.

"Teresita, this is Air Canada Crew scheduling calling. Did you get home ok?"

"Yes, I did. The police escorted me home, and the RCMP detectives are here with me at my home. What's your name?"

"Sorry Teresita, It's Gary. I have been asked to call and make sure that everything is ok. Also, I was advised that you have been placed on temporary leave until this matter has been resolved. You are asked to keep Flight Crew scheduling up to date with any changes in your situation and to speak with the crew scheduling manager when you call."

"Okay, Gary, I understand. Thanks for the call."

The detectives looked relieved and got busy setting up the equipment for both my cell phone and the home phone. I felt certain that the calls would come in on my cell, but Detective Sanders said they needed to have all bases covered.

After what seemed like an hour, Detective Avino said everything was all set. There were a series of black boxes connected by a lot of wires and connected to both home phone and cell. There was one main box that looks like a stereo receiver that was the center of the equipment. It had a series of blue lights across the face, and they were very bright. Detective Avino told me that the old days of having to pick up an extension were long gone. Everything that comes in on either the home phone or cell would be recorded in a digital format. They can listen in live on any conversation, but it would all be recorded for analysis later.

Detective Sanders then told me, "Ms. Li. I will be leaving these two detectives here in your home to monitor the situation. They will record all calls and assist you with any information, details, or procedures that we will need to try to trap the kidnappers into giving us more information. The RCMP will then coordinate whatever we learn with Interpol and the Chinese Secret Police."

"Please cooperate with the detectives and follow any instructions they give you. Even though we do not anticipate any local safety concerns, we will be having an RCMP police cruiser drive by on a regular basis," he said. He also told me that both detectives would be replaced periodically depending on how long this would take to resolve. I should also try to continue my normal routine, but try and stay at home until we receive the next communication.

"Thanks for all your help. I really appreciate your assistance and hope this nightmare will be over soon. What do we do now?" I asked.

"The ball is in their court." He said. "From the information you have given us, the kidnappers have your cell number, and they will call you with some kind of an update, and what they expect from you. Obviously, this will be the ransom demand and instructions on how it is to be paid. We need to know, however before any of this can be confirmed."

Now the reality of the situation set in, and I am getting really worried about how this was happening and what mess Dave has gotten himself involved with, in China. I warned him so many times that this was not a good idea, but he claimed that aviation was so backward in China that he could not pass up an opportunity like this. I wondered if he went too far this time. I tried to tell him that the Chinese have been in business thousands of years before any other nation and that they were not going to let a *'gweilo'* (foreigner) come in and tell them how to teach pilots to fly! This I felt, was a very bad decision on his part. I also wondered who he had pissed off so badly that they decided to teach him a lesson of his own.

I noticed the two detectives were just sitting at the kitchen table where the equipment was set up and not very busy. I asked if everything was ok.

Detective Avino says, "Yes, Ms. Li, this is where we sit around and wait. It's the hardest part of the job."

"Look, we may be here for some time together, so please call me Teresita," I said.

"That's probably a good idea. We are here to help, and you can call me Pem."

Detective Colson says, "Please call me Pamela or Pam. And Pem is right. We may be here for some time until you get any further information to have some sense of timing or deadline from the kidnappers."

"I'm so glad to have you guys here with me. It gives me some hope that this disaster can have some positive ending. I have a really good contact with the Canadian embassy in China, and he will be working on this as well. I have no doubt that he is stirring the pot in Shanghai and Beijing to get all the help he can from the Chinese authorities."

"That's really helpful," Pem says. "We are at a distinct disadvantage being thousands of miles away from being able to help move things along, so any help we can get from China would be a plus."

"If it's ok with you, I need to have a bath and try to relax."

Pamela said, "Please go ahead and take your time. Take your cell phone with you in case a call comes in, and we need to record the details."

I headed into my bedroom and got undressed and dumped my dirty flight uniform shirts in a bag to take to the cleaners. Dave usually irons my uniform jacket and skirt before a flight, and the thought of him, doing those little things suddenly brought me to tears. I made my way to the bathroom and ran a hot bath. My usual procedure is to decompress at least for an hour replacing the moisture lost in flight, and my body adjusted to the lack of high-altitude compression. This process was not helping today. I kept crying and not getting any relief from my normal routine. My eyes were red and puffy when I got out of the bath.

CHAPTER 7

Kidnapped location,
Somewhere south of Beijing
Monday afternoon.

Not sure of the time, but Albert arrived, what seemed like mid-afternoon. When he came in, he came right in my face and said, "How does it feel now when you were not in control of anything. I have your life in my hands, and when I am done with you, your visa will be canceled, and you will be kicked out of the country."

Then he spoke to the other three kidnappers, and they seemed to be having a discussion between themselves for quite some time. The Major who had come in earlier in the day and was in and out a few times was trying to tell Albert something that I wish I understood. I only had learned a few words and phrases in Mandarin in the time I was here in China. Cantonese seemed to be a harsher dialect and not that easy to learn as a foreigner. They made a decision, and Albert took out his cell phone and changed out his SIM card for another one. I was wondering what this was all about. Then he gave the phone to the Major. The Major took out a card from his pocket, looked at it and then punched in some numbers. He waited for what seemed like a long few minutes, and then someone must have answered.

He immediately spoke very rapidly in Cantonese. The conversation went on for some time. He then looked at Albert and said something very quickly.

Albert then came over to me and said. “Teresita has asked to talk to you. She wants to make sure that you are alright. You will only have a few minutes to tell her that you are ok. Do not tell her anything else. Where you were or who has kidnapped you! Understand me?”

“Don’t try to be a hero, or you will regret it.” He says.

“Okay, I understand.” I was hoping that I could say something that would tell Teresita who had kidnapped me and where I was. Unfortunately, I had no clue where I was, other than I was sure it was south of Beijing. Most pilots I know have this innate sense of direction that seemed built-in. Not sure if it’s a learned skill from years of flying or some talent we were born with.

I also wanted to give her some clue as to who had kidnapped me. I did not have any idea of what to say that would tell her that she knew who it was. I was now scared and felt completely helpless and at a loss for words. And this was doubly scary as it was one of Teresita’s friends that introduced me to Albert back in Vancouver a few years ago. I found myself hyperventilating and hard to breathe.

Then Baby Face went into the other room and came back with a rusty kitchen knife. He made a threatening gesture and ran the back of the knife under his throat and then pointed the knife at me.

This was too much to take, and I began to cry and babble like some crazy person. Not even sure what I was saying. Baby Face came over to me and then put the point of the knife in my right ear. I felt the pressure from the knife-point and not sure how to react, so I just kept still and hoped for the best.

“Don’t say anything other than you are ok.” He said.

At this point, I can hardly see through my tears and barely able to take in some air. The Major came over and handed me the phone but kept his hand on it as well.

Suddenly, I yell, "Teresita, I am okay, but you need to get them the money, or they will kill me!"

The Major yanked the phone away from me and started talking to Teresita. Then he punched the off button and hands the phone back to Albert.

Baby Face took the knife away from my other ear and smiled at me.

I can't believe what I just went through. I felt my ear where he had the knife but did not come away with blood, so I guessed he did not break the skin.

Albert then removed the SIM card and inserted another one. This procedure was just plain weird to me and not sure what the heck was going on. He and the Major had a lengthy conversation. Then he finally came over to me and said. "Well, that went off ok for you. We gave Teresita until Saturday to deliver the money. We told her to ask her brother to save you. He is a big millionaire and can easily afford the money. He goes to Vegas four or five times a year and always wins big. He has a lot of restaurants that were doing very well, so no problem there."

At this point, I realized my days were certainly numbered as her brother did not like me, and never really thought Teresita and I were a good match for each other. I knew right away that this was not going to end well. I started crying again.

Albert said. "Shut up and get over it."

I said I needed to go to the bathroom. Baby Face led me out to the filthy bathroom, and I had no option but to wash my face in the dirty water from the sink. I tried to make sure not to touch the sides of the sink, which looked like it was infested with bacteria and probably had not been cleaned in ages.

When Baby Face escorted me back into the bedroom, the Major and Albert left. The Major came back sometime later with a few plastic bags. He made the Ugly guy bring a small table in from the other room, which I guessed was near the front door. He opened the different bags and took out a bunch of cardboard takeout containers. I realized how famished I was and glad that the girls in the office had taught me about Chinese food and how to order.

Usually, in our office at lunch, we took a two-hour break during which time we spent one hour speaking English and one hour teaching me Mandarin. In the beginning, they ordered the food and explained what to order and what I might like to eat. I have always liked Chinese food, so this was somewhat different, depending on what you wanted to buy from the street vendors. Not always looking clean and germ-free, but mostly tasting great.

Then when they felt that I had learned enough Chinese, I was asked to go out and get lunch for the office staff and not to speak any English! This was a trial and error routine, and a few times I brought back some items that got everyone laughing. No laughing matter now, let me tell you.

The Major had brought quite a selection of food because he probably did not know what I would eat. However, he had fried rice, onion cakes, which I really liked, fried chicken, and a few vegetable boxes, none of which I even looked at. I hate vegetables of any sort, and most of them tasted horrible. Something from my childhood, I never got over.

All three of the kidnappers ate as well. Then the Major went out and came back a few minutes later with a bottle that looked like wine and some plastic cups. He and the other two idiots were smiling and had at least three or four cups each. Nobody asked me if I wanted any. Not that I would have anyway. Chinese liquor is, at best, a miserable tasting concoction that leaves you wanting to scrub your mouth with a brillo pad to get rid of the taste and the residue on your tongue.

After a few hours of drinking and talking, the Major left, and Baby Face told me time to sleep. Just then, his cell phone rang. He reached into his pocket and took out the phone and then said the usual Chinese greeting '*Nihao.*'

Then he listened. Someone on the other end was so loud even I could hear the noise coming from the phone. He eventually went into the front room and continued the conversation there. When he was finished and came back in the room, he and the Ugly guy had quite a shouting match. This was an interesting turn of events but not sure what to make of it.

Baby Face made me get into our sleeping position and went through the intricate process of inserting our arms into the jacket and zipping up the front until we were joined at the hip (not literally, but it sure felt that way).

I had trouble trying to relax and get some sleep, but any rest eluded me for hours. The Ugly guy was asleep in his sleeping bag right in front of the closed door and snoring like a hog! Baby Face was also sleeping very soundly, and my thoughts turned to possible ways to get away and escape from them.

Nothing came to mind. I thought about the back door that was hidden behind the curtain and wondered if it was possible to open the door and then get out that way. I remember the Major had made sure the door was locked but did not see him remove a key from the door. So, I was reasonably certain that the door could be unlocked from the inside without a problem.

Then, of course, I had to consider how to extricate myself from the jacket and Baby Face without him waking up. I kept coming up with reasons why this would not work and at some point, fell asleep with the problems unresolved.

Chapter 8

Teresita at home
Vancouver, Monday night
12 hours behind Beijing

I got up after a few hours of fitful sleep. I headed into the bathroom and did my due diligence and got cleaned up. My eyes were still red from crying, and I only hoped that today would shine some light on the problem.

I opened my bedroom door and saw two new faces sitting at the table. They both turned around and said hi.

"I am Detective Olsen, and this is Detective Lara Hamilton. How are you feeling?"

"I'm not exactly sure how I'm feeling, but thanks for asking. How long have you been here?"

"Well, we switched off about six hours ago. Detectives Avino and Colson will be here shortly to relieve us. Is there anything we can do for you?"

"Actually, there is," I say. "How about making this nightmare go away if I just go back to bed and wake up in a few hours."

"Unfortunately, that is outside our control, and we will have to just see it through to a safe conclusion for your husband." Detective Olsen says.

I asked if anything had happened since I went to bed, but they both shook their heads, and Detective Hamilton said, "If either phone rang, you would know about it right away. But we felt you needed your rest."

"Not sure if you could call it rest, but I managed to sleep for a few hours. I kept seeing bad things in a dream, so I hope it is not a sign of things to come."

Just then, the front doorbell rang. Detective Olsen says, "Please go back into the bedroom and let me check it out."

When he saw the police cruiser outside, he knew it was the relief crew. So, he told me to come out of the bedroom.

When the changeover was complete, I asked if they needed anything, coffee or tea. Detective Colson says they already had breakfast before checking in for work.

Pamela says, "Teresita, how are you this morning? Are you able to work with us to gather any more information? I'm sure the kidnappers will be contacting you again pretty soon with further instructions. We need to be ready with some responses to whatever they were demanding and to try to get them to make some mistakes that we can then use to have the Chinese authorities keep up the pressure to locate the kidnappers."

"Pamela, I am more settled this morning even though scared to death for what Dave must be going through. I think my aviation emergency training that I have had over the years have allowed me not to panic and to think about the situation in terms of resolving the issue. However, nothing in my 28 years of flying have prepared me for this one!"

"What is it you need to know that we haven't discussed already," I said.

Pamela looks at Pem and said quietly, “In any situation like this, we need to look at background details and try to find any possible connections that you may be aware of but not necessarily important enough for you to remember without prompting. We are going to start asking some questions that you may feel uncomfortable with at the beginning, but please try to remember that we are on your side and want to have this kidnapping resolved safely. I hope you can see that.”

“Yes, I understand. Where do you want to begin?” I asked.

“First of all, do you have any idea who might have been involved in this situation,” Pamela asks.

“I am totally clueless as to who may be responsible for this,” I said. However, I have been meeting Dave in China when I have my days off every five or six weeks. I usually spend a week with him, sometimes less and have met quite a few people he has met in his business start-up.”

Pem said, “Do you know anyone he may have met that could be responsible for this kind of criminal behavior?”

I thought for a short while and said, “Mostly we met with his staff in his office who were all young and very nice. There are four young women and one man, an Australian who is Dave’s lead instructor. And we also met with the Canadian Embassy staff on many occasions. They have been extremely helpful in getting him contacts with the officials at CAAC.”

Pem said, “What is CAAC.”

“They are the Civil Aviation Administration of China, similar to the Department of Transport (DOT) here in Canada and the FAA in the US.”

Okay, Pem says, “I got it. Why is he meeting with CAAC?”

"Dave's main goal is to set up a flight training school in China and teach young Chinese how to fly."

"Don't they have many other flight schools in China?" Pem asked.

"No, there is only one other government flight training institute in Western China, and they need a lot more flight training facilities as China's aviation industry is now becoming much larger, and they are requesting international routes to many other countries."

"Through the Canadian Embassy in Beijing, Dave has met with a few Chinese airlines and has made an offer to Shandong Airlines to train a lot of new pilots. Not sure if that will ever work out, but he is actively pursuing this airline and has met with them on many occasions." I said.

"Well, that is really interesting. Could there be other angry competitors because he is trying to get an agreement with a Chinese airline as a foreigner? That would make some sense. He could have upset some local group that wants to do the same type of business!" Pem said softly.

"I'm not really sure, Pem. I do know that the people in charge of transportation at the Canadian Embassy have been very helpful, and I have met his main contact there. A very professional Embassy official named Peter Parson. He has actually traveled with Dave to some of the Chinese airlines and made introductions to many of the airline officials and CAAC as well." I said.

Just then, my cell phone rang. Pem said, "Let it ring a few more times and then pick up."

All of a sudden, I feel a real restriction in my throat, and it was hard to breathe. Pamela got up quickly and came up behind me and rubbed my shoulders. I looked at the screen and didn't see a name, only a long series of numbers that I did not recognize.

"It's a long-distance number," I said.

The phone rang for another few times, and Pem said "Okay, Teresita, answer the call. Try to speak slowly and see if you can get a feel for who may be calling. Even ask for a name. You never know who is calling, and you want to know who it is anyway. Go ahead."

"Hello?" I said.

A harsh voice says *"Nihao"*

"Nihao ma. (Hello to you too- typical Chinese greeting) Who is this," I asked.

"Never mind he says in Cantonese. Just listen, and don't speak!" He said abruptly.

Pem and Pamela both have on their headphones and were listening to the conversation. Pem gave me a hand signal that told me to get the conversation moving. I noticed the recording box has its lights flashing and probably recording as well.

The rest of the conversation is in Cantonese. Here was what he said.

"We know you are back in Vancouver. We are watching your house. You must not contact the Police or any other agency, or we will kill your husband!"

"Listen carefully to these instructions. The ransom is Five Hundred Thousand US Dollars. The money must be paid by Saturday this weekend, or we will kill your husband."

"We will call you again to make sure you have the money and then tell you how it must be delivered. There must be no delay, or we kill him if we do not get the money."

"Do you understand?" The man said angrily.

Pem made a gesture telling me to ask to speak to Dave. I tell the man. "I need to speak with Dave. I want to know he is okay."

"You do not tell me what to do." He says. "I tell you what to do."

Suddenly I feel very strong and tell the man. "If I don't speak with him, how do I know he is still alive?"

There is silence on the phone for a few seconds and then muffled as if someone put their hand over the speaker.

Then I hear his voice. "Teresita?" Oh my God, I need to get out of here. I am still ok, but they were telling me that if they don't get the money by this weekend, they will kill me." He sounded terrified.

I couldn't even speak. My emotions were so raw, and I wanted to cry and laugh at the same time. At least he was alive! I started to shake, and Pamela made a soothing gesture to say calm down and try to relax.

I finally get the courage to ask. "Who is doing this to you? Do you know these people?"

Silence on the phone. The harsh voice says, "He does not know anything, and if you ask that question again, he will be beaten badly, just to teach you a lesson."

I froze and didn't say a word. I was so upset I hit the off button on the phone. I now start crying, and hot tears were rolling down my cheeks. I was trembling with rage and more afraid than ever.

"They say I must not go to the police, and they are watching the house," I screamed at Pem.

"Easy there, Teresita. If they were really watching the house, they would have seen all the police cruisers for the past thirty-plus hours, both on the driveway and at the front door. They are obviously not watching the house. Try not to let this drive you crazy. You did very well on the call. We now have proof that this is a serious international kidnapping situation, and more resources will be made available."

That did not make me feel any better, but somehow I was able to calm down somewhat. I head to the front window. But all I can see is the police car out front. I turned back to Pem and Pamela and said. "Are you certain they are not watching the house. When I was in Shanghai on my layover, they knew which hotel I was staying at, and that had me really scared."

Pem's phone rang and he got up and went downstairs into Dave's office. He was down there for some time. Pamela asked me if I wanted something to calm my nerves. I put on some water to boil and made a pot of Chinese tea for both of us. The normal routine of boiling water and steeping tea leaves made me feel a bit more normal.

Pem finally came back upstairs and said, "Teresita, I have some news for you. Because the phone call was international, the case has now been escalated to top priority. The RCMP called Interpol and asked for their assistance. As you know, Interpol is an international law enforcement agency that investigates all types of criminal activities around the world, and this definitely qualifies under their mandate."

I said. "What does that mean?"

Pem says. "Interpol will be our international liaison with the Chinese police authorities and will be assisting us in any way they can." Since we are thousands of miles away from the source of the kidnapping, this will be a great help in finding and prosecuting the bad guys."

I sat down at the kitchen table and began to calm down. Pamela came over and massages my shoulders. She said, "It's ok to cry. This is a highly unusual situation, and I completely understand. You must be really stressed out. We are here to help you get through this ordeal. Please try not to hang up on the kidnappers next time they call."

"I'm certain they will call back. I know how the Chinese think." I said.

Chapter 9

Kidnapped location,
Somewhere south of Beijing, Tuesday
12 hours ahead of Vancouver

Some time in the morning, the same routine. Baby Face unzips the parka and we separate ourselves. Dull sunshine was coming through the curtains at the end of the room. He got off the bed and I noticed the Ugly guy was not in the room, and the door to the front room was open. As I wondered what was going on, Baby Face makes a loud pissing noise in the toilet, and I realized that I needed to go as well. When he came out, I told him I needed to take a leak, and he told me to go ahead.

I opened my small bag that Albert had brought with my medication and took out my toothbrush and toothpaste. Before I headed into the toilet, I saw a few bottles of water on the small table where the remains of cardboard food containers from last night and the empty wine bottles. I grabbed a bottle of water and took it with me into the toilet. As I passed through the doorway and turned into the toilet, I noticed the Ugly guy sitting on a brown dirty looking couch in the front room. He looked up and made a motion to Baby Face to keep an eye on me.

I took a pee and then turned to the filthy sink and trying to not touch any part of it, I brushed my teeth and used the bottled water to wash and rinse my mouth. Since I have not really had a good meal since Sunday midday, I did not have the urge to use the toilet to take a shit.

I headed back into the bedroom with Baby Face as my escort. All of a sudden he got in my face and said, "Your woman better get us the money or you die this weekend. I kill you myself," he said with a nasty grin, showing me his discolored teeth with a gap in between the front two.

I tried not to react to this insanity but felt the walls closing in on me. I got back on the bed and tried to read. The words had no meaning at this time, but at least I was trying to keep my spirits up.

Sometime later in the morning, the Major arrives and the three of them had quite a discussion between themselves in Cantonese. The Major was obviously in charge of this group of thugs. Anyway, after the discussion, he left, and I heard the front door slam.

Then the Major and Ugly guy came back into the bedroom. They didn't say anything, and I wondered where Baby Face was. He was the only guy who spoke good English and the only one I spoke with normally. I felt the Major knew some English but with a heavy accent. He did not speak to me directly. After a couple of hours, I realized that Baby Face had left with Albert and wondered what that was about.

There was a knock at the front door. The Major went out to get the door. He talked to someone, and then I heard two voices talking at the same time. Shortly after, Baby Face and the Major came back into the bedroom. Baby Face had a sly smile on his face like he just swallowed a canary! Then the Major told them something and left the room. I heard the front door slam.

He returned in what felt like an hour with more plastic bags, and this time he brought a case of bottled water. The food was the same type of street food you could get on any Chinese street. The vendors were all the same. They had a small stand, usually made from old furniture crates and even some metal sheets. They cooked over an open flame, and usually, everything they sold came from the one frying pan or wok. Nothing would get washed, so you took your life in your hands when you bought this type of food.

By this time, I was really hungry and didn't care if I got sick or not. Chances are I might not live to see this weekend, so I was more concerned about my present state of starvation and hunger pains. I filled one the paper plates with two of the meats, not quite certain what they were, but one tasted like lamb and quite tasty. I piled on the ever-present onion cakes and fried rice. I hated any type of vegetables so left those alone.

While we ate, there was not much conversation between the three kidnappers. Then Baby Face's cell phone rang. He picked up his phone from the table and headed into the front room. After a couple of minutes, he began shouting. The Major left the bedroom and went into the front room. After a long time listening, Baby Face made a few remarks, and then I guessed he shut off his phone.

Then I heard the Major telling him something. I heard the same phrase over and over. Only much later would I find out what this about, but right now I was clueless. They both finally came back into the bedroom, and Baby Face looked like he had been chastised, and the Major looked very angry. He talked to Ugly man, and I could tell he was relaying some information about the phone call.

Nothing more was said for a while. Then a knock on the outside door. The Ugly man went and opened the door, and I heard Alberts voice.

When he came into the room, he looked at me and said, "We have your Canadian passport. Once we get the ransom your visa will be revoked and you will be kicked out of the country, never to return. I warned you right at the beginning that I have a lot of *'guanxi'* in this country so I can do anything I want with you."

All at once I realized that I was in real jeopardy. How in God's name did he get my passport? I kept my passport in my desk drawer in the office with $1,500 US dollars, 5000 HK dollars, and some Chinese yuan, somewhere around ten thousand. The rate of exchange is $1.00 US is equivalent to 700 Yuan.

I wanted to ask how he got my passport, but I was now scared to ask and find out that my staff in the office had been injured or worse. These guys were really connected.

Albert said, "I got your passport, money, laptop, and some other stuff from your apartment."

Again, I wondered how they got past the security at the apartment building. Visitor entry into the building was all well-regulated. This also told me that they were able to avoid any issues regarding security, and I was really concerned for my office staff and their well-being.

He then spoke to the Major and took out his phone. He went through the same procedure as before. He took out the SIM card, inserted another SIM card into the phone, and punched in a bunch of numbers. He waited for some time and then suddenly handed the phone to the Major.

The Major started talking. He sounded quite menacing, and he was obviously trying to intimidate someone on the other end of the line. He spoke some more, then covered the phone and spoke to Albert. They yapped for a couple of seconds in Cantonese, and then Albert thought for a few seconds then spoke to me in English. I was amazed by the ability of anyone who can talk and think in two languages without missing a beat. Simply amazing.

"Teresita wants to talk to you. Remember what I said before. Say nothing else other than you are okay."

Since I was not expecting this at all, I felt some sense of hope. I nodded my head and told him that I would not say anything else. He gestured to the Major to give me the phone. Baby Face ran into the other room again and came back with the same rusty kitchen knife. He grabbed my head and said, "You fuck up, and I will stick this right in your ear." He held the sharp point of the knife just inside my right ear. I felt like pissing my pants but tried to keep my cool.

The Major handed me the phone. When I tried to move my head, Baby Face pulled me back to him and grabbed me around the shoulders while he kept the pointed end of the knife in my ear. I could actually feel it pressing on my skin but not enough to draw blood.

I held the phone up to my left ear. "Teresita. Oh my God, I need to get out of here. I am still ok, but they are telling me that if they don't get the money by this week-end they will kill me."

The Major grabbed the phone before I can say another word. He barked some comments in Cantonese to Teresita, and then apparently, she must have hung up on him. He handed the phone back to Albert, who went through the same routine of removing the SIM card and reinserting another SIM card. I was still mystified by this process and kept thinking about it but came to no conclusion.

The Major told Albert something and Albert got mad. He yelled at me. "She hung up! She must want you dead! What's wrong with your wife?"

At this point, I was speechless and really started to worry about the next revelation or whatever these guys had in mind. It was not long in coming. Albert and the Major went into the front room and closed the bedroom door. Not sure why this was necessary as I didn't speak Cantonese and only understood a few words in Mandarin.

Since I didn't have my watch, I could not tell how long they were in the other room. But, it was probably more than half an hour at least.

When they came back into the bedroom, Albert immediately said. "I know you have a bank account in a local bank, and I want the account numbers and any pin number you have for withdrawal of money."

"What!" I said, "You must be crazy if you think you can get into my bank accounts!"

"Listen up you, jackass," Albert said. "I am going to do more than that. When you leave this country, you will be broke and penniless. And if we don't get the money and the ransom it won't matter anyway, as you will be dead."

"Well, good luck with that mate. Because I am a foreigner, I was not allowed to set up a local bank account in Yuan so the bank accounts for paying staff and expenses have all been set up by Olivia. She is the only person who goes to the bank each week to do any banking. So, I guess you are out of luck."

Albert looked at me for a few minutes and then said, "I know Olivia is your office manager. We will get her to go to the bank and withdraw the funds."

"And how were you going to do that? You don't think she will know that something is very wrong and contact the police? She is a pretty smart woman, and I'm sure you will not be able to put anything over on her. And she knows that you and I have not been talking to each other for a long time."

"I guess we will just have to kidnap her and take her to the bank to make the withdrawal," Albert said with an evil grin.

At this stage, I felt that these assholes must be total idiots. To even consider that they could kidnap someone and then take them to a bank and withdraw money was the height of stupidity. This began to give me a sense of hope that something could actually transpire out of this bank situation that could help free me. All of a sudden, my mind is running in all directions. What if this could be used to get some information to the Embassy, the Chinese police, and even the guys I met through the Embassy officials with contacts back in Canada.

I realized that Albert was now looking at me with suspicion. I looked up from the bed and saw him thinking about how to get more money. This guy was all about money and influence.

He tried to use me to get connected with the Film Institute of Vancouver to become their accredited partner in China. He was able to convince me to do this early on in our supposed business relationship. Due to my sitting on the Board of the Canadian Association of Career Colleges, I was able to meet the CEO of the Film Institute, and the Institue allowed me to represent them in China for a limited time period.

The plan was to include vetting young Chinese students who wanted to enter the film industry to enroll in the Canadian Film Institute in Vancouver, which ran many programs for film, video, and producing animated ads from scratch. A very successful film organization in Canada.

Albert unfortunately, went so far as using my contact to advertise in China for anyone interested in the film industry to contact him as he represented the Film Institute of Canada. This was total hogwash, but since he did this all in Chinese, I was completely unaware of his duplicity and intent.

It was only Olivia who was my office manager that broke the news. She told me that Albert was in fact conning young Chinese students to pay him for enrollment fees, pay for visa applications to Canada, and to write a test to achieve a Canadian Certificate from the Film Institute.

At this point, we were sharing office space, where I kept all of our important documents in a small safe in her office. Unknown to both Olivia and me, Albert was able to unlock the combination to the safe and remove the blank certificates I was issued by the Vancouver Film Institute. He then forged my signature and used them to influence these students to pay him enrolment and visa application fees.

Once I found this out, I told Albert that our budding business relationship was over, and I was never going to do business with him again! I remembered him being very upset at the time and now realized just how devious this guy really was.

I decided to make a new start and moved to a new location office on my own. I also kept Olivia as my Office Manager. She was a very bright your woman, honest and completely bi-lingual or probably tri-lingual. We moved to our own office located in a section of Beijing where foreigners were allowed to open and set up my Company – Global Institute of Technology (GIT).

Now I was faced with a very disturbed individual who felt he had the upper hand and out to destroy my life and steal my livelihood. I really underestimated this devious and mentally unbalanced criminal character. And now, I was probably going to pay for this with my life.

How was Olivia going to handle this situation? I was now worried for her safety and the other girls in the office. I was not as worried about Brian, my lead instructor. A nice Australian dude. I knew he could take care of himself in any situation.

Then I started going back over the situation and how I got into this mess on Sunday. I had just returned from a trip to Hong Kong on Friday after being away from Beijing for a week on my usual monthly business trip to conduct banking and have a meeting with my accountant.

As a foreigner, I was not allowed to open a local business account in China in US dollars, and could only open a business account in a Chinese central bank thus necessitating regular trips to HK to transfer money for payroll and business expenses in Yuan to the Beijing account when required and usually requested by Olivia. She handled all the payables and invoices for my company.

Chapter 10

Olivia, GIT Office Manager
Office of Global Institute of Technology (GIT)
Beijing, Tuesday morning

Olivia sat at her desk and pondered the situation. The two other office staff had not arrived as yet, so the place was very still and quiet for this time of day. She kept busy for a while and then walked back to Dave's office just to see if he had come back late last night. He usually was the first one in the office every day. So not having heard from him since Friday was somewhat concerning, but not bothering me very much.

Nothing had been disturbed in his office, and his desk was as usual, clean and organized. The way he wanted it. He hated people especially Jennifer leaving paperwork on his desk without telling him what the reason was. He kept reminding both girls that was what inboxes were for. And this morning there was nothing in the out tray either. A sure sign Dave had not come in and worked over the weekend.

I heard the office door open and heard heavy footsteps and knew that Brian had arrived. He must have seen the light in Dave's office, and my coat hung on the coat rack by the front entry.

"Olivia, good morning. Are you alone?" Brian asked.

"Morning Brian. Yes, Dave is not in and I was just checking to see if he came in over the weekend, but there's no sign that he did. Have you heard from him?"

"No, he didn't say anything about his schedule for this week. There was so much activity since he got back from Hong Kong late Thursday, I was expecting to see him here really early and get an update."

"That surprised me as well. While he was away last week, we had so many calls from potential students I was hoping we could talk about scheduling a meeting with them. And also plan for another meeting with CAAC regarding the flight school program accreditation." I said.

"I agree with you, Olivia. It is getting really busy and we need to have a meeting with these prospective students and assess their English language capability."

"I guess we will hear from him this morning and then we can plan the student interviews. What bothered me was the last person who came in on Friday and sat in the waiting area for almost an hour. She said that she was waiting to meet with Dave, but I had not scheduled any meeting for Friday morning as he had just returned from Hong Kong late Thursday."

She did not give me her English name either, which I thought was rather strange. She did not look like our normal student applicant. She seemed to be in her late 30's or somewhere there. She sat out there and just looked at the various flight and flying magazines on the coffee table." Olivia said.

"I did not pay her much attention when I went to the kitchen to get another coffee. However, you are right, she looked a bit older for a student wanting to learn to fly." Brian said quietly. "They are usually in their late teens or early twenties and most of the time, their parents or at least one parent accompanied them to the interview."

"Anyway, I have a lot of work to do on the student visa applications to Canada to work on, so don't have a lot of time to worry about her. Maybe this was one of the contacts from the Embassy that they recommended and gave her the office address." I said.

"That's probably it. I have lots on my plate as well," Brian responded.

Brian headed into his office, and I sat back down at my desk. The paperwork for each student visa to Canada was very comprehensive, so I got started. We received almost forty applications from potential student pilots after Dave's visits to the Aviation University in Tianjin. This was a great start and hopefully, we can arrange visas for all of them.

Jennifer and Sandra arrived almost at the same time. We talked a bit about their weekend and then I had to cut it short to get my work going. Sandra is supposed to be translating part of GIT's flight attendant training program from English into Chinese. This was to encourage some of the Chinese airlines to use our training program for their employees.

So far, it's a lot of grunt work and not much progress to show as yet. I know Dave had high hopes that this would be a good program to sell to China Eastern Airlines and possibly China Southern. Jennifer is now working on vetting the initial student enquires and taking calls for Brian and Dave. She has been acting as our receptionist. Her English was pretty good, and she speaks Mandarin, Cantonese and a few other local dialects.

Suddenly the door opens, and a young chubby Chinese guy comes into the office. Usually, people tend to knock on the door first. But this guy just comes right in and stands in front of my desk. He looked like a friendly guy and smiled at Sandra and then said to me, "You must be Olivia," He said.

"I am Stan, and Dave made sure I spoke to you about what he needs. He had to make an emergency trip to Hong Kong over the weekend to speak with his accountant and the bank about something pretty important regarding visas for Canadian students." Stan said.

This guy spoke pretty good English and smiled a lot. I gave a few thoughts as to why Dave did not tell me about any emergency trip to HK. I know he goes there frequently to coordinate banking arrangements with Canada as he can't set up a commercial bank account for our company in China as he is a foreigner.

The guy said he was going to meet with Dave in Hong Kong. He said he works with Dave's Accountant as a courier and regularly traveled to HK, Shanghai, and wherever the accountant's firm had clients.

This made some sense to me, and I was not worried about any of this. Dave's business travels took him to many parts of China regularly and mainly to Hong Kong two or three times a month.

"Tell me what files he wants, and I'll get them for you," I said.

"I need to show you what he needs," Stan said.

"Okay, I guess you know what you are looking for." We headed back to Dave's office, and he immediately began looking through the top drawer of the desk.

"There are no files in there. They are usually in the big file drawer at the bottom." I said.

Stan said, "I know that, but he also needs his passport for the rest of his trip. He is going to Zhuhai and Fujian to meet some other airlines."

I am a bit concerned at this point I but don't say anything. He grabbed Dave's passport. There is an envelope he always carries with him that has money in various currencies as it's quite difficult to get any local currency when he travels to smaller cities in China. US dollars also helped pave the way for cooperation.

He then opened the bottom drawer and just grabbed a handful of files that Dave had put together from his initial meetings with the Major Chinese Airlines.

I said, "Are you sure you have the right files?" Stan didn't answer right away and now seemed anxious to get out of the office.

"I'm pretty sure I have what he needs. Thanks for your help. I know Dave will appreciate your cooperation." Stan then leaves the office hurriedly. The office door closes as he headed for the elevator.

I now began to think about this situation and decide that perhaps Brian could make some sense of this.

I walk over to his office and said, "Brian you got a minute?"

"Yes, Olivia, What's up? By the way who was that guy that just left the office. I haven't seen him before. Is he from the building maintenance?" Brian asked.

"No, apparently Dave is in Hong Kong for an emergency meeting with the accountants. What bothers me this guy who is a courier for the HK accountant, wanted some files but he also took Dave's passport and the envelope that Dave keeps with all the different currency he needs when he travels." Olivia says.

"Wait a minute, Olivia. Dave can't be in Hong Kong without his passport! He never travels anywhere, even in China, without his passport and local currency. Something doesn't sound too kosher about this. Do you know anything about this guy? Dave needs his passport even to get into Hong Kong."

Oh heck, Brian! I never thought about that. I have only traveled outside of China once many years ago and traveled on a travel permit valid for only one trip. I never had a passport. If you are an unmarried female under the age of twenty-eight, you will not be allowed to travel outside of China unless the government approves of the reason and issues a travel permit. The brain drain out of China by females is enormous, and the government is trying to stem the tide of young women leaving the country."

"I really hadn't given that much thought," Brian said. "We need to get ahold of this situation now. When did you talk to Dave last?"

"I only saw him on Friday morning for a few minutes when he met with that student that was waiting for him. Then he went to lunch with one of his Embassy contacts and did not come back to the office."

"Why don't you call the HK accountant's office and see if they know what this emergency meeting is all about and see if you can talk to Dave," Brian said anxiously.

"Okay, let me do it now," I said. I went back to my desk, and because I didn't normally contact their office, I took a few minutes going through my contact list to find the right number. When I called the office, I spoke with their receptionist, who said that Dave had just left their office last week Thursday, and no other meetings were scheduled for this month! She checked with the two CPA's that took care of GIT's business, and neither one said an emergency meeting was planned.

Suddenly, I got really worried. I hurried back into Brian's office. "Brian, there is no emergency meeting in HK at the accountant's office, and they have not seen Dave since last Thursday."

"Okay, Olivia. Let me handle this. I am going to call the Canadian Embassy and talk to the guys that Dave usually sees when he goes over there."

I went back to my desk and started crying. Jennifer looked over from her desk and said, "What's wrong, Olivia?"

"I don't know," I managed to get out through my tears, but Dave might be in trouble, and I made a mistake by letting this guy take his passport and money out of the office." I cried some more and then headed into the washroom to try to compose myself. I only hope that this turns out to be nothing serious.

Brian was waiting at my desk when I got back from the washroom.

"Well," he said, "we have a huge problem. Dave has been kidnapped. The security officer at the Embassy had been informed since Sunday night, and they have also alerted the Chinese police and their foreign affairs department." Brian said with a grim look on his face.

"Oh my God, Brian. Is he okay? Where is he?" I said.

"Nobody knows anything else at this stage, Olivia. They asked us not to talk to anyone and not let any documents leave the office. They also want to talk to anyone who calls the office looking for him. The Embassy security, which is actually a detachment of the Royal Canadian Mounted Police (RCMP) and responsible for the safety and security of Embassy personnel, is also charged with handling any suspicious matters regarding Canadian citizens living in China." Brian told me.

Jennifer and Sandra are both crying, and I realized that I had to be the strong one. Brian hugged each of us and asked us to try and stay calm and let the authorities handle this matter. Brian then asked me a few questions about the guy that came into the office and took Dave's passport and files. I tell him what little I knew, and I felt it was my mistake that I let this happen.

"Listen, Olivia, this is not your mistake. The kidnapping took place apparently sometime on Sunday, so you had no idea what was going on. Don't beat yourself up over this. I know how great the Embassy officials are and they will not rest until he is found. My wife works at the Australian Embassy, so I know something about their routine when some disaster like this occurs. Maybe you should take the rest of the day off and try not to worry too much."

I couldn't take any time away from the office. I had so much work to get all the student visas applications completed and then getting all the payments for the medicals and the fees for the flight training. That was the last thing I wanted to do. I needed something to help keep my mind off this terrible situation.

Brian came out of his office a few minutes later and asked me how I was doing. I try to put a brave face on and said, "I'm okay. I will stay and work anyway. I don't want to be alone at home and worry. I feel better if I'm here at least and helping to keep the office going."

Brian says, "If you want to stay busy that's fine. If you feel you need to talk to someone, at least, let me know or come and talk to me."

Chapter 11

Kidnapped location,
Somewhere south of Beijing
Later Tuesday afternoon/evening/night

Late in the afternoon, and the only way I could guess the approximate time is that the sunshine had dissipated, and it looked as if night was setting in. I had no concept of the time passing, and this only heightened my fear and premonition that this was not going to end well for me.

I was now also worried about Olivia and rest of the office staff. From what Albert had said, they had planned this very efficiently and knew what they were doing. This only made the situation ever more dangerous for me, and everyone around me.

Before Albert left, he took a handful of yuan from my envelope that had my travel cash and told them something. They all laughed and looked at me. I'm not sure what this meant, but somehow, I was the butt of the joke.

Albert and the Major left together. The Major returned with a whole new set of plastic bags, then went back out and returned with some more bags. After Ugly man set the containers on the table. He opened them up, and we all dug in. I filled my paper plate with the usual, fried rice and fried chicken. I didn't touch the vegetables or soup.

Once we got finished, Baby Face collected the unfinished food containers and the dirty plates and took them out to the front room. Not sure if there was a garbage container there, but the place could not smell much worse than it did right now.

Then a strange thing happened. The Major opened one of the other bags that he brought with him. He opened one and took out a large box. When he opened the box, I saw it had a small ceramic pot, much like a teapot, and several smaller ceramic cups each in its own recess.

Next, he opened another bag, took out a container of tea leaves, and dumped it into the pot. He opened another bag and took out a large thermos usually seen in most Chinese offices and used to make tea for office workers. He filled up the pot with hot water from the thermos and covered the pot. While we waited for the tea leaves to steep, he handed one of the smaller ceramic cups to each of the other two thugs.

Then he looked at me and offered me a cup as well. He made the unmistakable gesture to take the cup. And I did, without knowing what was going on. Then weirdness happens again. He poured out a small portion of the hot liquid into each of the three cups and then one for himself.

He then made a move that, again, was unmistakable for having a toast! What is going on I wondered? Anyway, Baby Face said, "drink up. This is a toast to you. You bring much good luck to us, so we toast you! And it is your money that bought this tea set, so drink up and enjoy." I managed to drink the tea, and, since I came to China began to like the various types of tea the Chinese consume on a daily basis, sometimes three and four times a day.

I couldn't believe this. Several thoughts ran through my head at this time, not the least of which is that this group of idiots were truly insane, and I had to find a way to get out of this prison cell. No one was going to save me.

The Major opened another bag and took out two bottles of wine. He opened the first bottle and poured some into their three cups. He did not offer me any wine. They talked and laughed with each other while they finished the bottle. The Major opened the second bottle, and they proceeded to finish that one as well.

Once they finished the second bottle, the Major left just like he had the past two nights, and we prepared for sleep. We did the same routine again with the parka, and Baby Face and I were joined by the zipped-up jacket.

This was one sleepless night. I couldn't even turn or move in any direction as I was virtually tied to Baby Face by the sleeves of the jacket. But all manner of thoughts invaded my mind. Most of them trying to make some sense of how I got involved with China in the first place.

While I was working at the Vancouver airport office of my good friend, who ran an air cargo operation, this whole mess got started. I was helping to supervise his cargo operation while planning and developing my flight training programs. I began to unravel how all the signs were missed. I was in fact sharing the cargo office while setting up my international training operation. I called it Global International Technology or GIT.

I had intended to pursue training Chinese young people who wanted to become airline pilots. My background in aviation spanned over twenty years of expertise, both mechanical as well as flight and ground training. I had high hopes of pulling off something that had only been dreamed of by lots of organizations. Unfortunately, I had not considered how important it was to have enough support in terms of personnel and finances to stay the course.

I felt all this expertise was a sure-fire way of opening an international flight training school in China, which was short of flight training facilities and was entering a new phase of aviation thanks, in part, to the prospect of hosting the Olympics in 2008.

I really missed the concept that there is no way a foreigner could be successful at opening and running a flight school in China. I needed my head examined. Too late for that now, I feared.

Now my thoughts went to how I met Albert. This is what was so shocking to me in hindsight. Teresita, who was always supportive of my plan to train pilots in China, actually was the one who had introduced me to Albert through a very good friend of hers. Her friend had explained that Albert was in Vancouver and looking to connect with someone in the film industry.

Since Teresita knew that I was on the Board of the Canadian Career Colleges, she figured that I would know somebody to introduce him to. She called me at the office and told me his name. I agreed to meet, and he came out to the airport office.

Now that I was going over everything in excruciating detail, I realized that Albert was a con man, and I was completely duped in this entire process. My own fault for not looking deeper into his background. He wowed me into believing that because his father was a retired governor of a province in China that he had great *'guanxi'* in the country and if I helped him with his film project, that he could connect me with all the right people in China, especially CAAC, the Chinese Aviation authority.

Sometime late in the night or early morning, I finally fell asleep. When I awoke this morning, I knew that the plan these thugs had was not going well. Everyone seemed on edge and tense. This was now day four of this really bizarre operation. I was also feeling the strain of being held against my will for any length of time. Until I was kidnapped, I never ever considered how you would deal with not being in control of yourself or your surroundings. I found it rather frightening, to say the least.

Wednesday morning
Day four

The same procedure as before. Unzipping the jacket, then getting slowly out of the bed after Baby Face had gone to the toilet. The morning routine completed, I brushed my teeth and consumed two bottles of water before getting back on the bed. I was getting tired from having to sit or lie on the bed for all these hours. Not even allowed to stretch my legs or walk around the small area except for a few steps to the toilet and back. Baby Face insisted on my staying on the bed at all times. At least they did not tie me up or restrain me to the bed.

Ugly guy looked even more dangerous this morning. He scowled at me, and I realized that perhaps he had a hangover from all the wine they drank last night. He and Baby Face did not say too much to each other either, so I knew this was getting to them.

Early this morning, I guess around eight o'clock or thereabouts, the Major and Albert arrived within minutes of each other. They took Baby Face into the front room and had a heated discussion for some time. When they came back into the bedroom, I was grateful as they had left me alone with Ugly guy who looked like he wanted to do me some harm, and I was increasingly worried about being left alone with him.

Then Albert repeated the same procedure with the SIM card and his phone. He made the call, and I knew by this time he was calling Teresita in Canada. Once the phone was answered, he handed the phone to the Major. The Major immediately spoke very quickly, and it sounded like he was demanding answers. He paused a lot after a short speech and then listened for the response. It obviously did not please him, and he raised his voice.

The next thing I knew, he looked at the phone in his hand, and then turned to Albert. He made an angry remark to Albert, who got red in the face and shouted at me. "Your crazy woman hung up the phone."

"She must really want you dead." He said.

I started to panic and had the urge to pee right then. There was no way I was going to say anything to make matters worse, so I closed my legs and hoped I could keep it in. And, I did not want to give Baby Face an excuse to ram the knife in my ear. Which I am sure he was hoping to have the opportunity to do.

Albert then talked to the Major for a few minutes and then gave him back the phone after punching in the phone numbers. Then he said something to the Major that sounded pretty ominous. Not knowing what they were talking about was really scary.

The phone was answered, and the Major began shouting immediately. He shouted into the phone for a couple of minutes and then listened. He made another comment just as heated as before and then shut off the phone. Albert changed out the SIM card again and put the phone away.

"We are going to make some changes. If the money is not delivered by Saturday, we are taking you somewhere else until we decide how to get the money from your bank. We are going to force Olivia to go to the bank on Saturday and empty your bank accounts. And if we don't get the ransom, you are going to regret screwing up my deal with your life and possibly Olivia's as well."

"You really are going to go through this crazy plan to get Olivia to go to the bank on Saturday?" I asked incredulously. These guys were absolutely bonkers.

"Oh yes," Albert says, "we have plans for you either way. With or without the ransom."

I now realized the end is in sight, and I was worried about what Teresita was going through in Vancouver and how to try and save Olivia from this deadly situation now getting out of hand. *How was this going to end,* I wondered with resignation and a heavy heart.

Then Baby Face's phone rang. They all looked at him and started talking. He picked up his phone and headed into the front room. He stayed there for quite some time, and it sounded like he was arguing with someone. The other three talked quietly among themselves, and I really wondered what the heck was going on in there.

When he finally cut off the phone call and came back into the room, they all started talking, and he answered angrily and then fell quiet. I didn't know what to make of this until much later.

When Albert left and was followed by the Major, maybe an hour later, I pondered the enormity of the situation. And this now hit me really hard. They had no intention of letting me go! Either they got the ransom, or maybe even if they get that, they will still kidnap Olivia and make her withdraw all the GIT money in our accounts. This really scared the crap out of me. At the end of this, they would dispose of both of us in some godforsaken hellhole.

As the day wore on, I felt desperation setting in. I now felt that I must somehow try to escape from these animals, or they would certainly kill me this weekend.

So, I started thinking of any means possible to escape. I am not a very passive person in any way, but not crazy or aggressive either. These men were much more than just kidnappers. I was now aware that at least two of them, the Major and Ugly man had military training and suspected the Major may still be in some active role. Especially as he left for hours at a time and then came back as if he was returning from duty due to his dress and mannerism. He always seemed to be giving orders to the others, and even did not take it kindly when Albert told him something.

I now took stock again of the interior of the bedroom. I looked around the dingy bedroom trying to spot anything that might be used to get my freedom from these thugs and this place.

I focused my attention on the far wall with the curtain. This was the only exit that I saw as a possibility. I knew there was a door behind the curtain as I saw the Major check it the first night we came in. Pretty sure I did not see him remove a key, and perhaps that was the only way to escape and freedom.

The only other option was through the bedroom door, which was a non-starter, as that was where Ugly man slept in front of, and actually touched the door with the sleeping bag when he was in it. And, before he set the bag down for the night, he locked the door and put the key in his pocket. So, no way out that way. And of course, I couldn't fight these thugs. They had already proven their strength many times over the last few days.

Then I took stock of what I had with me. Little or nothing. Then I remembered my travel bag with medication and some personal items for layovers. It also acted as my pillow when I tried to sleep at night. I carefully opened the bag and took out my overnight bag, and took out a couple of bottles looking like I was checking my tablets. In reality, it allowed me to glance around inside the bag and lo and behold, I saw a small nail clipper! This filled me with some faint hope.

While putting the pill bottles back in the bag, I palmed the nail clipper and removed it. It was now difficult to put it under the bag as I placed it back on the bed. Since it had been my pillow since Albert brought it with my medication, neither Baby Face or Ugly man said or made me do anything. I felt they did not see anything. I lay back down on the bed and tried to calm my thoughts.

I was now resolute in my decision. I had to try to escape and tonight was the night. Tomorrow night might be too late, and who knew what would happen Friday or the weekend. It would have to be tonight.

Chapter 12

Teresita at home
Vancouver, Wednesday night

Today had been very stressful. A house full of police officers and neighbors knocking on my door asking questions. I couldn't tell them what going on, as this would be too much for me to handle. The house was on a corner and very visible, the police cars were very much evident. I put them off as nicely as possible and closed the door. The two detectives were very understanding and tried to make me feel that things would turn out all right.

They don't know the Chinese mentality like I did. They tended to treat foreigners like dirt and didn't care who they hurt.

I worried that Dave had gotten himself involved with a group of people who wanted nothing more than to have a foreigner like him come in to start a business and then try and take it over. I wondered if that is what was happening here. I had not told my brother or sister what was happening. I didn't want to start another conversation about this disaster. It was bad enough for me, without getting other people's opinions involved.

Thanks to my emergency aviation training, I felt more in control of my emotions today. I now felt I could deal with this situation, but not sure how this would help Dave as there was no way I could come up with half-a-million US dollars for the ransom.

The detectives were both sitting at the table and Pamela had been talking to the national RCMP contact for international and foreign affairs and looked at me and smiled! I wondered what that was about. When she got off the phone, she was very excited and said to me and Pem. You are not going to believe this."

"Because Interpol has established a link with China and the RCMP office in Ottawa, they are getting some updated information. They are asking to keep the kidnappers talking as long as possible in order to try to identify where the call is originating, and if possible, the Chinese Secret Police (CSP) will be tasked to find the location."

"Apparently the Chinese Secret Police intelligence organization is doing everything they can to find the location. They are monitoring any international calls to Canada but, up to now, have not managed to track or identify any calls that may be the kidnappers." Pamela says.

I got a bit excited myself and hoped that this was some sign of things to come. We talked over a few scenarios and Pem asked me if I would talk to my brother about putting up the ransom. He needed to know, as the RCMP might be able to cover the delivery of the ransom and, in cooperation with Interpol and the CSP, recover the ransom when they catch the kidnappers. Pem told me this would be a joint effort and I should at least see if it was possible to raise the money as it would most likely be returned.

I told him my brother might be a millionaire, but he was not one of Dave's supporters. "I am not going to ask him."

We sat and waited for what seemed like a really boring time. I ordered some Chinese takeout, and when it was delivered, we were quiet while we ate. Once we had finished, I put all the leftovers in the fridge and the empty containers in the trash. Just as I finished up, I sat back down at the table to watch the news on TV.

My cell phone rang, and I jumped. *Oh my God, is it them?* I went to pick up the phone, but Pem put his hand on mine and said, "Don't pick up right away, let it ring a few times."

I got very nervous but did as he asked. He nodded his head after a few more rings. I finally picked up, and my hand was shaking. I noticed it was an international number.

"Hello." I said.

"Nihao" I heard from the same voice I heard before. Pem and Pamela were looking at the recording unit, and blue lights were flashing, and they both had their headphones on and were listening intently.

He spoke very quickly, and I had trouble keeping up with his Cantonese accent. He was demanding that I tell him I have the money, and we would need to have the money transferred by wire to a bank account in Beijing.

I was so upset I could barely talk. I told him, "Why didn't you kidnap someone with money. Are you crazy? I don't have all the money and need more time," and I cut off the call.

Pem jerked the headphones off and said, "Teresita, how could you hang up on them? You know we need to keep them on the line for as long as possible."

"I know," I said. "I just lost it there for a minute. But they will call back, I'm damn sure."

They both glared at me and shut off the recording device. No sooner than Pamela turned off the machine, the phone rang again. I waited for a couple more rings and then picked up. I notice it's the same number.

I whispered to Pem. "I told you they would call back."

"Nihao" I said.

The same voice in rapid-fire Cantonese angrily tells me if I hang up again, they will kill Dave tonight. I try to tamp down an angry retort and respond with, "I need more time. I only have some of the money and cannot get any more for a few days."

He said I had no more time, and the money must be transferred to China before Saturday. He said that they were not going to wait any longer. He shouts, "Send the money now." And cut the call.

I hit the off button slowly and realized that I was holding my breath. When I let it out, Pamela took off her headphones and came around the table and gave me a hug. I held onto her and began crying. "What is going to happen now," I wailed.

Pamela said, "Try not to get too worked up over the call. Even though you scared us when you hung up on them, we think you kept them on the phone as long as you could. Did they say anything else different than the last call?"

"Not really, only that they want the money wired to a bank in Beijing. I wonder how that is supposed to work! Do they really expect to go into the bank and withdraw that kind of money?"

Pem says, "We were only one part of this operation, Teresita. We have to wait and see what transpires from this call. One good thing. An international call will not be able to be hidden from Interpol or the Chinese Intelligence Service. I'm sure someone is on to this as we speak."

My home phone rang. I wasn't sure, but it couldn't be the kidnappers. They didn't have my home number. I answered, and it was one of my friends who lived a few miles away. I tried to say hello and get off the phone, but she wants to know how I was doing. I wasn't sure what she meant, and then she said, "Your house showed up on the front page of the local Chinese newspaper." There is a story that suggests that your husband has been kidnapped in China, and the picture shows the house on Panorama Drive.

"What's going on, Teresita? Is this true? My God, what is going on?" Audrey said.

"I'm really sorry Audrey, I can't talk to you right now. I am right in the middle of trying to deal with this situation, so I hope you understand."

"Of course, Teresita. I hope you are okay, and I hope that everything works out for the best. Call me when you can. God bless you and Dave."

I put down the phone and started crying again. I couldn't deal with this much longer. I only hoped that this would be over soon. Even though I wanted him safe, I couldn't wait to see the end of this. I headed into my bedroom and fell on the bed. Pamela came in after me and said they were leaving for the night and the new shift will be taking over. She felt we wouldn't hear from the kidnappers again tonight and I should try to get some rest. She said they would be seeing me in the morning. I heard noises as the second crew took over, but I didn't come out of the bedroom. I didn't feel I could talk to anyone right now.

I cried until I ran out of tears. Then I washed up in the bathroom and took a sleeping pill. I fell into a restless sleep and very weird thoughts invaded my mind until sleep mercifully took over.

CHAPTER 13

Kidnapped location, Somewhere south of Beijing
Late Wednesday Night

As the night wore on, I felt the anticipation taking hold of me. I needed to make my move tonight and have to get started somehow. The three thugs drank more wine again earlier and I hoped they were sound asleep. The Major left a few hours ago and I waited until Ugly man started snoring on the floor next to the door.

Baby Face and I were still joined together by the sleeves of the parka. But now I had the comfort of the small nail clippers under the bag and felt for it. I finally made contact with it and hid it in my right hand. My left hand was in the right sleeve of the parka, and Baby Face had his right arm in the left sleeve.

Once the parka was zipped up, we had virtually no movement. I began moving around like I was restless, and after a few times, Baby Face goes back into a fairly deep sleep. No doubt helped by the copious amounts of wine he drank when they finished off the last bottle. He also snored intermittently, so I could gauge when he was fully asleep.

Once he began snoring again, I started slowly making up my mind what steps to take next. I slowly unfolded the nail clipper and pulled out the file with a sharp end to it. I rubbed my fingers over the edge, and then the enormity of what had to happen next stopped me in my tracks.

In order for me to escape from Baby Face, I have to stick this sharp file in his neck and then cover his mouth with my hand. But then reality sets in. How do I stick this in his neck with my right hand as my other hand is trapped in the sleeve of the parka? I would not be able to cover his mouth and prevent him from screaming. A sure-fire way of waking up Ugly guy and having him kill me immediately.

Time stood still as I pondered my next move. I stayed perfectly still for a few minutes and considered my options. Slim to none. This was not going to work as I had thought.

Then I remembered the predicament I was in and with no solution on the horizon. This was either up to me or death at some point in the near future. Not much to choose from. So I made a decision. I would extricate myself from Baby Face and try to make an escape through the back door behind the curtain.

I took a few deep breaths. Ever so slowly, I started to pull my hand out of the sleeve and immediately realized that I couldn't complete this move without unzipping the parka. I reached for the zipper and paused to make sure Baby Face was sleeping and lightly snoring. The Ugly man was also snoring, so the quiet sound of the zipper would not be heard, I hoped.

I slowly eased the zipper little by little until it was about halfway down. This gave me enough play to enable me to move my left arm up through the sleeve. I gently pulled until I felt my arm clear the collar of the parka and then pulled my hand into my body. This felt like heaven. Baby Face was still snoring away, and I felt step 1 was successful.

On to step 2. Getting off the bed. This was not as easy as it sounded either. The only way for me to get off the bed was at the bottom of the bed. Baby Face was taking up the only open side away from the wall.

I considered my next moves carefully. Once I got off the bed and got to the door, I would be committed to escape, and whatever came next, I would have to deal with. I remembered that the Major put most of the empty wine bottles on the floor near the door, so that was another obstacle I had to avoid.

I couldn't take my small travel bag as there was nothing in it that could help me in any way. I could feel my heart beating like crazy. My thoughts were jumbled, and I was nervous and scared as heck. I took a few more deep breaths before I committed myself to move. I realized that I was still holding the small nail clippers in my right hand but was afraid to let it go.

I now knew that nothing was going to happen unless I made a move. I began to inch my way down the bed ever so slowly. Now that I was free of the restrictions of the parka, I could move more freely. I finally got near the foot of the bed and paused to see if any of the two suspected anything.

All was quiet. Both thugs were snoring. I couldn't see much from where I was. I saw a faint bit of light coming through the curtain that was covering the door and window area. I wasn't sure if it was moonlight or some partial light from a street lamp.

This gave me a shadowy glimpse of the floor. I was now partially standing with my back to the bed. I tried to see where the bottles were located and tried to plot a path to the door. I only had socks on, and now I began to appreciate the pickle that I was in. How would I navigate if I made it outside? It was still a cold spring in Beijing. I remembered only a few days ago when I came back from Hong Kong. It was colder than a witch's tit!

Now I slid across the dirty floor towards the curtain and the door. I carefully stepped over a couple of wine bottles and got to the curtain.

I grasped the edge and gently pulled it aside. Oh, Christ! The door actually did have a lock and a deadbolt. The deadbolt required a key to unlock it. This was a real bummer.

I silently moved aside the curtain next to the door. The dim light from a possible street lamp now exposed two or three dirty windows that have vertical bars securing any access to the windows themselves. No way around that either. I took stock of my present situation. No exits anywhere. I definitely couldn't take on Ugly man at the bedroom door.

At this point, I saw no possible escape route. I sighed to myself and decided not to make matters worse. I'd better get back on the bed and assume the original position. Maybe another opportunity would present itself.

I stepped gingerly back around the bottles and quietly made my way back to the bed. The return trip was frustrating and frightening. I was now very worried that either one or the other would wake up and catch me out of bed. I froze for a few seconds while I considered the implications of getting caught. Not sure I was any worse off now if either Ugly guy or Baby Face would wake up.

I made it back to the bed and slowly pulled myself up backward as there was only a small space between the wall and Baby Face. Not enough to turn over. So I inched my way back up the bed to approximately where I was before. I then had a hard time finding where to insert my left hand into the right sleeve. I felt around feverishly and managed to locate the opening near the collar.

The problem was that Baby Face had shifted during my absence and the reason I had a hard time finding the opening. Once I got my hand all the way down the sleeve, I had several panicky moments trying to zip up the parka. I finally left it stuck somewhere near the top, but close enough, I felt.

I didn't sleep again for the rest of the night. It passed agonizingly slowly. Thursday morning dawned. It did not look like a good start to my day. I am fearful of what events this day would uncover.

Chapter 14

Olivia – GIT Office Manager
Office of Global Institute of Technology (GIT)
Beijing, Thursday morning.

I was now in a full-blown state of panic. No one had heard from Dave. I had not spoken to anyone else who might have any more information on the situation.

Brian contacted the Canadian Embassy again yesterday and was told that everything was being done to try to find a safe solution to this huge issue. He was told that there was a lot of cooperation between Chinese police agencies and the Canadian RCMP. They told Brian to cooperate with any of the Chinese authorities responsible for foreigner's safety.

After the office staff arrived and we talked among ourselves, we realized that this situation might be more serious than the Embassy understood. Jennifer, who came from another province in the Western part of the country, said kidnapping was a regular crime in her home province.

I said, "have they kidnapped foreigners before?"

Jennifer said, "I'm not sure. All I can tell you is that this is a regular occurrence, and very rarely were the victims found alive."

We talked about this some more, and then Brian came out of his office and told us to try and keep our minds off this problem and get back to work.

We did our best and settled down to our normal routine, even though nothing could ever be routine again. The morning seemed to drag on, and the phone calls and phone interviews took their normal boring process, sometimes to a positive conclusion. Not very often, however.

I now worried about Dave, and my tears started to fall. He was not only my boss. He was also my good friend. He had taught me so much about the aviation business that I was really thankful we met. When Teresita came to the office the first time, I think she felt that Dave and I were more than friends. We went out to lunch a couple of times, and I was able to convince her that Dave had always been a gentleman in the office and would never compromise his working relationship with the staff.

I also remembered telling her that I traveled with Dave on many of his business trips to meet with the airlines and acting as his interpreter. He had protected me on a few occasions when some airline executives felt it is customary to have sex with the boss's assistant since he must be doing it as well. I told Teresita that that would never happen, and she should not worry about Dave. He was a gentleman through and through. He had even told me some stories about some of the women who applied to work for GIT and came on to him, just to get the job. They had probably never met someone like him.

Even some of the potential students who wanted to become pilots leaned over and rubbed their breasts on his shoulders when he is showing them some specific detail in a manual. It was so funny to watch.

I knew how hard he was working to try to start a flight school in China and train many young people for different careers in aviation. He had formed GIT to make a difference, and I only hoped he would succeed.

Older Chinese parents did not understand the growing Chinese aviation industry and worried about the safety of their children in this new career. A valid point, as aircraft crashes in China were many and often deadly.

We were still getting many interested applicants on a regular basis. They were all looking at learning English, the international language of aviation around the world. This might be our biggest challenge. I was still thinking about all the obstacles we had to overcome when there was a knock at the door.

It opened, and two men came into the office. They were both dressed in identical blue suits which did not fit either of them well. Both were wearing white shirts and black ties. A sure sign these were some type of government employees. They were probably in their mid-thirties to early forties. One was older and clean-shaven with short grey hair and a serious facial expression. The younger one had a small beard and small black eyes that were really penetrating. No smiles on either face.

"Nihao" I said. (Hello)

"Nihao Ma", the older one said. "Are you the office manager," he says in Cantonese.

"Shi de," I said, "Who are you."

He responded in Cantonese. "My name is Detective Ban Lok, and this is Detective Li Chin."

He took out an official-looking badge, and so did his partner. "We are investigating the kidnapping of a Canadian citizen. We understand that this is his company, and he works in this office."

"Yes," I say. "Apparently, my boss, the owner of the company, Dave Rohee was kidnapped here in the city last Sunday."

Brian had heard the conversation and came into the reception area and asked me. "Hey Olivia, what's going on? What do these guys want?"

"These are detectives from the Chinese foreign Affairs department. They are investigating Dave's kidnapping."

"Well, it's about time somebody got off their asses!" Brian remarks.

Detective Ban Lok said,' "We speak English. No need for that kind of language. Who are you?"

"My name is Brian Donavan. I am the Lead Instructor for the company." Said Brian.

"Well, Mr. Donavan. We have been on this investigation since Monday night, so please show some appreciation for our efforts on Mr. Rohee's behalf."

"Okay, I apologize for my attitude. We are all pretty upset by the whole episode and feel left out of the loop." Brian interjected.

"And I can appreciate the stress of not knowing if your boss is alive and safe. Please let me advise you that we are doing everything we can to resolve this matter safely. We don't take kindly to foreigners being kidnapped in our country." Detective Lok said.

"What we would like to do is talk to each of you about any events or anything out of the ordinary over the past week before the kidnapping or after."

I instantly remembered the guy who came on Tuesday and took Dave's passport and some files. I told them exactly what happened that morning. They were both very interested and asked lots of questions.

Detective Chin pulled out a radio and barked into it. He was asking one of his men to find the building manager and see if there were any cameras in the building. He waited while Detective Lok spoke to Jennifer and Sandra.

While he was talking to Brian, Detective Chin's radio squawks loudly. He turned it down and then hurried out of the office. He said something to Detective Lok over his shoulder that sounded like there might be a video security recording. This was a somewhat normal procedure for foreign companies operating in China. They were only allowed to have a licensed company business address in specific locations, and I had always assumed that these addresses were all recorded or videotaped. Perhaps this could be good news for them to identify at least one of the kidnappers.

We were anxiously waiting for Detective Chin to return and tell us if they were able to identify anyone in the video. Nothing happened for another 45 minutes.

Detective Chin finally came back into the office and shook his head. "We got the video and have been looking at it several times. We managed to locate the time when a person you described came off the elevator and approached the office door."

"Unfortunately, the quality of the video is very bad, and we are not able to identify anyone specifically. However, the entry camera on the main floor was able to capture his image when he was leaving, and he got into the passenger side of a black car. Not sure what make it was, but I will be taking the videotape down to our head office and run it through our database of known felons. We now know there is more than one person involved. Hopefully, we can get an ID that we can put a name to." Detective Chin says.

The two detectives left the office. We breathed a sigh of relief. This had been a strain on all of us. At least we knew that the Chinese police authorities were investigating the kidnapping. The rest of the day passed with no further news.

Chapter 15

Kidnapped location,
Somewhere South of Beijing
Thursday Morning & Afternoon

I opened my eyes, even though I hadn't slept a wink. I was now very restless and having gone through an emotional up and down of a fruitless escape, I was drained of emotion. I couldn't even raise my head off the travel bag. I had placed the nail clippers back in the bag once I was back on the bed and immobile next to Baby Face. The morning seemed dark and gloomy. It might only be my dark thoughts that were forcing my outlook on this possibly, next to last day before they decide to get rid of me.

I was pretty sure there was no way any ransom would be paid. And I failed to see how it would be possible to force Olivia to go into the bank on Saturday morning to withdraw all the company funds. It was the most ridiculous idea I had heard yet from these jokers. I wondered if they were playing with a full deck.

This morning, Baby Face's phone rang again. He picked up the phone and headed into the front room to talk. This did not accomplish much as he began shouting immediately. If I could understand the language, I could know who he was talking to and what he was talking about. While he was on the phone Ugly man was not a happy person, and I could see him getting more and more upset with the way the conversation was going.

When Baby Face was finished, he came back into the bedroom, and he and Ugly man began arguing. It went on for some time and both of them were so angry, I thought they were going to have a fight. Eventually, they both calmed down. Some time passed with great tension between my two captors. They were not even talking to each other.

There was a knock on the door, and Ugly man went to get it. The Major came into the bedroom and spoke to Baby Face in an angry voice. I could tell he was not a happy camper and pretty pissed at Baby Face.

There was another knock at the door. Albert had arrived. Then after a lengthy discussion, Albert, Baby Face, and the Major left. I was now left alone with Ugly guy. This did not make for a comfortable situation. I was now very concerned, since he did not speak any English, and I did not speak any Cantonese.

A few hours passed. I was lying on the bed trying to read the one book I had in my travel bag. The book named "Hostage" by Robert Crais, very accurately depicted how I was feeling as a kidnap victim. It came as quite a shock when I saw what book it was. I always kept at least one book in my travel bag and another one in my laptop bag in case of travel delays. These were usually softcover paperbacks. Not very easy to find English paperback books except at international airports or large book stores in Hong Kong.

My mind was not really focused on reading as it was in a turmoil over why I was left alone with one thug, and the only English speaking kidnapper (other than Albert) had gone out with the other two. I remembered that the Major also knew some English but never really spoke it unless giving me an order. He was most definitely someone in authority accustomed to giving orders and having them obeyed.

The Major and Baby Face returned, without Albert, sometime mid-afternoon with a bunch of plastic bags smelling of food, bottled water, and two more bottles of wine. They sat down in the rickety folding chairs that were always in the front room and brought them into the bedroom when we were eating. I always sat on the edge of the bed. No chair for me.

The rest of the day passed with not much being said. It appeared that they were waiting for something to happen. I was sure it wasn't a phone call as no calls were made unless Albert was present and always used his phone. The SIM card routine was bothering me, and only much later, I was able to find out why this was so important.

Albert never showed up on Thursday afternoon or evening. The Major and the other two started drinking wine pretty early that evening. I was nervous, and my stomach kept acting up, no doubt due to the uncertainty of the next day or two. I was using the filthy toilet more than normal, and Ugly guy was starting to get suspicious of my needing the toilet so frequently. As soon as I asked to go, he came and stood outside the toilet, and since there was no door, just kept staring at me with daggers for eyes.

The rest of the evening my mind kept playing tricks with my subconscious and rehashing the various negative outcomes that were likely to happen on Saturday. I was now quite certain that no ransom was forthcoming and no one to save the day. Nothing like reality to make one face one's final destiny. Was I scared to face this? Never being in this situation before, I had no training or previous knowledge of kidnappings that ended without loss of life. Everything I had read indicated that they almost always end in someone's death, usually the kidnapped victim. In this case, that would be me.

I did my best to try to go through the routine of getting ready for bed. Not sure I succeeded but since there were no other options, I tried to put a brave face on the situation. Zipped up with Baby Face and tried to get some sleep. Another restless night and very little sleep.

Chapter 16

Teresita at home
Vancouver, Thursday Afternoon/Evening/Night

When I got up late today, I had a bad feeling and could not stop the tremors in my hands. I threw up all the breakfast I ate, could not face eating lunch, and wandered around the house aimlessly.

Pem and Pamela tried to make me feel that everything was being done by all parties in China, Ottawa and linked through Interpol.

I got a call from operations at Air Canada. They were asking if I had any idea when I would be available for flight operations. I told the dispatcher that the company was aware of my present situation and he should have some notes on his computer. He said the note was there but did not give him any more information other than I was not available for crew scheduling due to a personal family problem.

I tried to have patience with him. His name was Brad, and obviously for security reasons the company did not want to release any more details, which, now that I think about it, made complete sense. If the reason was stated in the crew notes, my phone would not stop ringing all day and all night. I had lots of friends in the airline that I had known over the twenty-eight-plus years working as a flight attendant.

Brad asked me to call dispatch and give them an update as soon as I knew a return-to-work date. I agreed and hung up the phone. Pamela asked me if everything was ok at work. I told her the company had been very cautious about what was written in the crew scheduling dispatch notes. She agreed that too much information would tend to confuse the situation.

It is getting fairly late in the evening, and we have not had a call from the kidnappers. This was somewhat of a concern as I was supposed to talk to them about how to wire the money. The money that I didn't have. Detective Sanders came by earlier and asked how I was holding up. When I told him, the walls were starting to press in on me, and he said to try to keep a positive attitude that everything will work out for the better.

He said that both Pem and Pamela had told him how calm I seemed to be, and I had provided them with enough information for Interpol and the Chinese Secret Police, who were now involved in trying to identify who the kidnappers were and how to trap them. When he left, I decided there was nothing more I could do, and only hoped that events would work out to Dave's benefit and safe return.

Chapter 17

Kidnapped location,
Somewhere South of Beijing
Friday morning

Friday morning dawned like the previous four. Miserable and daunting. A little weak sunshine illuminated the room from behind the curtain. I was probably foolish to imagine that they would leave an exit unsecured. I was almost positive that this group had conducted this type of criminal activity before and in this same location. It seemed tailor-made for them to have someone locked away without any prying eyes or suspicious neighbors.

Not that I knew what the surrounding area was like. I could only assume from the unkempt and disheveled appearance of the inside of the place what the exterior might present. Not a happy situation to find myself in. Not knowing in what condition the rest of the adjoining buildings might be like, they could probably spirit me out of here without anyone being the wiser.

The early morning passed as boring as the previous days. The two thugs, Ugly man, and Baby Face were very tense, and I guessed the end game was making them just as nervous as I was. Of course, since I was the main victim in this melodrama, I was more frightened than ever.

Then there was a knock on the door. All of a sudden, Baby Face got up and almost ran to answer the door. Ugly man makes a gesture to me. It looked like he wanted me to stay on the bed and not move.

Where does he think I could go? I wasn't sure what to make of this. I wondered if this was something they had expected this morning.

Then I realized that this was the day before they were going to get Olivia to go to the bank! Oh crap. What next, I feared. There was some hushed conversation at the front door. It sounded like the Major's voice. Then a shouted sentence. The Ugly man answers. The door shut. Baby Face does not come back into the room, so I worry anew that they were on their way to kidnap Olivia. Were they going to bring her here?

This was by far the worst situation I could have ever considered for either of us.

Now I glanced at Ugly man. He did not seem, in any way, concerned about anything. But then over the course of the last four days, he had not been overly concerned about anything that had transpired. He seemed to be the perfect stooge boy for the Major and had little to say about any of the events that had taken place.

Time passed slowly. I couldn't even feel my heartbeat. I had been taking my blood pressure medication every day as usual. I was sure that my blood pressure was sky high right now. I had a constant headache since yesterday that would not go away. I no longer had any Tylenol #3, that would normally help reduce the intensity of the pain, so I had to suffer.

This was probably a lot less suffering that I would have to endure for the rest of today and whatever time I had left tomorrow. I try to meditate but could no longer seem to be able to clear my mind and focus on my breathing. I wondered why? My thoughts ranged far and wide.

I thought of my mother in Toronto, half-blind with cataracts in both eyes, my sister, who was the only caregiver my mother had. In addition to keeping her job, it was almost a full-time job taking care of our mother. I wasn't how she did it and managed to keep her Job. She had my undying gratitude.

I thought about my kids, all grown up and living their own lives, not knowing or possibly caring what happened to their old man. They might never know the extent of love and affection I had for them. Thanks to my not always letting them know where I was, or what I was doing, they might never know the truth.

I was ashamed of the way I had behaved these last few years. I had closed myself off from my family. Not for any specific reason, but merely to keep me from sharing my hopes and dreams. I have had so many in my lifetime. When we get to a point like this in our lives, we look back and ask why did we act so selfishly? At least that is what I was now doing. And I was not proud to admit the many mistakes I had made in my quest for success.

At least I would have tried to accomplish most of the goals that I had set out for myself in life. I made some and lost some. In the end, we only have ourselves to be the judge of our actions. My grandmother, "King Granny," our nickname for her, used to always tell me. "Don't be afraid to try. If you dream, dream in color. Try your best and always be honest with yourself."

Well, Granny, your words mattered all my life, and if this was the end of it, then at least I have tried my best. I am now teary-eyed as I pondered what might well be my last day on this earth.

I had so many visions of things that could have been but were not. Things that I could have changed but did not. I knew now I would never have the chance to rectify any of that. And this was not a pity party I was having with myself. Only the people that have experienced the worst in their lives could relate to this.

Friday Mid-afternoon, same location

There was a knock at the door. I dreaded what I feared I would see. When Ugly guy went and opened the door, I quietly stepped off the bed and peeked around the doorway. I heard voices first. Then Baby Face and the Major came in. I quickly pulled back into the bedroom and jumped back onto the bed.

All three came into the bedroom. No one looked at me. I tried to look at each face to see what type of expression I could glean from them. They were all pretty stoic and serious. The Major had a different look than the previous afternoons. Not sure what his look meant, but I was sure it was nothing good for me.

They had a fairly subdued discussion between themselves. I did not see any expression that told me anything specific. I fully regretted not learning more of the Chinese language, Cantonese, or Mandarin. My big mistake and obviously, too late to correct that now.

The next few hours passed agonizingly slowly. I could almost count the minutes. It's so boring. Nothing said. It looked as if they were waiting for something or someone, so I guessed they were waiting for Albert to arrive.

Early Friday Evening, same location

After what amounted to some more boring time passage, the Major got up and left the room. I assumed he was heading out to pick up dinner and more wine.

He said a few words to the other two, then walked away. I heard the front door close. All was quiet for a few moments. Neither of the two thugs said anything. A few minutes passed in silence.

Then I heard a knock on the door and figured the Major forget to tell them something.

Baby Face headed out of the bedroom towards the front door. As he opened the door, all hell broke loose!

The door banged open! There were several heavy noises and many voices shouting. I couldn't tell what was happening in the front room.

Ugly man moved through the doorway into the front room. As he moved, two figures dressed in full black outfits jumped onto him and slammed him to the floor. A third one was trying to help hold him down on the floor. He was resisting like a madman.

Then another figure ran into the bedroom and threw himself on top of me. I struggled to breathe.

He shouted in English – "You're safe, You're safe. My name is Henry, don't worry, I have you covered."

I tried to get out from under him. He says in my ear. "Don't move. Once we have them restrained, I will get off you."

Then I noticed that there was fighting going on in the bedroom and outside in the front room. Lots of harsh words and shouting. Heavy noises of hitting and slapping. I peered under Henry's arm and saw three men in black struggling with Ugly man. They have him pinned on the ground. He is fighting them with everything he has. Feet, hands, and head butts. To no avail. His opponents were just as strong as he is. And there were three of them. They finally were able to get handcuffs on him. One of the men then hit him on the head with a short piece of wood like a Billy club. Ugly man immediately goes quiet.

There was still lots of noise in the front room, and I could picture something similar happening to Baby Face.

Henry then got off me and said, “Okay, we have everything under control. You can get up now.”

As I got off the bed, I cried with relief. Then the truth hit me like a brick. I was saved! Oh my God, this was really happening. I couldn’t believe this was actually happening right in front of me.

There was still struggling and muttered words, which I am sure were curse words, some punches were still being thrown, even though Ugly man is fully restrained, he is now groggy from the hit on his head, but still trying to get free of his captors, to no avail. One officer was sitting on his legs and another one had an arm around his neck. The third one helped to hold him down. There were lots of voices yelling and shouting in the front room and possibly in Cantonese. So loud I couldn’t tell the difference.

I now realized that these men in black were not exactly what I would have assumed to be police officers. Even though they were all wearing similar black clothing, there was something very different about them. I was still in a state of shock, so not thinking very coherently at the moment.

Henry was still holding me by the arm and actually holding me up. Not sure I was stable enough to stand on my own. I was still crying with relief. He pointed to the bag on the bed and said, “Is this yours?”

I looked back at the miserable bed where I have virtually spent all of five days and began shaking. Henry pats me on the back and assures me, “Everything is ok, Mr. Rohee. You are safe, and we are taking you out of here now. Please take the bag.

I then noticed that Henry was holding a gun in his other hand. I realize that when he jumped on me he was holding the gun in one hand that he kept well above his head. It never registered in my mind until now. It now dawned on me that he was the only one with a gun. The others used their fists and Billy clubs. And they look like a well-trained group of men. All serious and mean looking.

I grabbed the small bag, and Henry pulled me along with him out of the bedroom. What met my eyes stunned me. There were seven or eight other men in black in the front room. Baby Face was in handcuffs, and two of the officers were each holding one of his arms. The others were looking at me and I saw a couple of smiles on a few faces. None of them spoke to me.

As soon as Baby Face saw me, he cried out in English, "Tell them I am good guy. I keep you alive. I not hurt you."

This had me crying again, and I was still shaking, now more angry than afraid. I couldn't even begin to think of what to say to this asshole. Henry pulled me towards the front door.

Baby Face yelled at me. "Tell them I not hurt you. I keep your camera bag safe for you. Here it is."

At the mention of a camera bag, I stopped Henry and turned around. Baby Face pointed to the broken-down couch on the back wall and pointed to an orange camera bag just sitting there in a corner. I now knew for sure that this was my camera bag, and Henry told one of the officers to bring me the bag.

When the officer handed me the bag, I unzipped the top and see my Nikon SLR and two extra lenses. I didn't look any further and grabbed the bag to my chest. I now had my travel, and my camera bag clutched to my chest with both arms.

Henry barked a command to his men. Two of them near the front door answered him. He then proceeded to hustle me out of the building. As we exited from the front door, I took notice of the immediate area.

There was a small area with another door opposite the prison I was in. It looked like an adjacent apartment. Henry turned left, and a few feet away was the front entrance to these two apartments.

It led us outside onto a dirty pavement about twenty feet from the street. There were many black sedans parked out on the street and lots of men in black standing around. I now see that they were all wearing black jackets with some Chinese lettering on the back. I assumed it must be a law enforcement agency. There were so many that I couldn't begin to count. Probably well over twenty or even thirty. I was so confused at the events that just transpired that I was not thinking properly.

Henry rushed me to the first sedan directly in front of the apartment. He opened the back door and quickly let me get in. He closed the door and told me to roll down the window. When I did, he said, "I'm just going to give some instructions to my crew, and then we will leave here."

I must have mumbled something as he turned and headed back into the apartment. When he went in, I finally got a chance to see where I had been held for five days! The place looked like a desolate backwater in some out of the way location. The apartment where they kept me was at the end of a multi-unit complex. Very run down and dirty exterior. One level with a few dirty windows to the street, garbage and old plastic bags blowing around in the blustery cold wind of early evening. There was no grass in the front, only a mix of dirt, gravel, and some sparse brown weeds dotted the area.

Now that I was able to see the surrounding area, I realized that if I were to escape, I would probably have been worse off as I had no idea of where I was. There was no familiar landmark, and I did remember that we drove for what seemed like hours before I was taken out of the car.

In a few minutes, Henry came out and got in the front passenger seat. Another officer got into the driver's side, and we took off. Henry said we had about a thirty-minute drive. When I asked where they were taking me, he said, "We are taking you to the nearest police station in the area."

When I asked where we were now, he said, "We are about an hour south of Beijing." This got me crying again. I couldn't seem to stop, and this is now embarrassing to be constantly sniveling like a kid!

When I had a few minutes to calm down, I asked Henry, "Can you tell me how you knew where I was."

Henry said, "Mr. Rohee, lots of people have been looking for you. Your Embassy, Interpol and Canadian Royal Mounted Police have all been involved in trying to find you. However, the agency that finally located exactly where you were being held, is the China Secret Police. The CSP has been monitoring all the phone activity from the location since Tuesday. You must be a popular person.

"Not really," I said. "I am just an average businessman trying to start a business in China. I now worry about all the publicity surrounding the kidnapping and any fallout that may affect my business in a negative manner."

All the while we were driving through a pretty desolate area with only a few people out and about. Not a lot of commercial businesses or strip malls, something that Beijing had in great numbers. We were obviously still outside the mainstream of Beijing and its environs.

Henry got on the radio and began speaking very rapidly in Cantonese. He spoke for some time. There was quite a bit of back and forth conversation. When he put down the mike, I asked him what that was all about.

He wasn't quite willing to answer, but after I asked him again, he said, "We are just making sure that all the kidnappers are accounted for and on their way to the station."

I asked him, "How may kidnappers did you catch?"

"We got all three of them," he says.

"What three," I said. "There were five kidnappers in total. Four men and one woman."

Henry turned around in his seat and said to me. "How do you know there were five.?"

"Tell me who you caught," I said.

Henry said quietly, "The ringleader named Albert, and the two we just caught when we rescued you."

"Then you missed one man and the woman who led me into the trap to be kidnapped."

"Okay, Mr. Rohee, when we debrief you at the station, we will get your full report and then take whatever action is necessary to catch the rest of the kidnappers. Try not to worry about that right now," said Henry.

Then I asked what police unit he represented, and he said that this group was specially trained to deal with hostage incidents, rescues, and something like a SWAT team in the US but not armed. They were used mainly in covert situations for takedowns that were not the culmination of an armed standoff. These men, he said, have various martial art skills and had been trained in different countries.

We drove for maybe another half-hour and pulled into a police station situated on a corner with a unique facade that looked out onto three streets. The front of the building had a wide set of stone steps leading up to the front entrance. The front steps actually faced the corner, and two of the three streets were visible from that vantage point.

The driver parked on one side, then he and Henry got out of the car. Henry came and opened the back-seat door and let me out. He guided me up the steps. He then said, "Stay here for a few minutes. We need to get ready to take the kidnappers into the building and prefer you not have to deal with seeing them again."

I agreed and he had me standing just outside the main glass doors with my two bags clutched to my chest. For a few minutes, I felt ok. Then after 10 minutes or so, I began to feel uneasy and very exposed. There was no one else around, and for a police station, I felt this was really strange.

Then a van and a few black sedans drove into the same parking lot but farther away from the main entrance. I felt very naked here all by myself and wondered who had just arrived.

Then the sedans disgorged a lot of men in black, and I realized that these were some of the same men that saved my ass from the kidnappers! What was going on here? I couldn't see the side of the van where the doors opened, so I had no idea who was in the van.

The men in black surrounded the open door of the van, and then took what looked like a couple of men out of the vehicle, and around the far side of the building. This freaked me out. I started shaking again. I was now seriously worried about my safety.

Then I saw a uniformed policeman pass by the front door. I quickly hurry to the doorway and when the glass doors opened, I shouted. "Hey, you. Get Henry, Get Henry."

Even though I knew he did not understand the language, he certainly got the message and hurried away. Just a few minutes later, Henry came running up to me. "What's wrong," he said.

"I am scared to death Henry. I am all alone out here and feel very unsafe. Can't you find somewhere for me to stay rather than out here?" I said, trembling with emotion.

"We did not want you inside for the same reason, Mr. Rohee. But I can understand how you are feeling. Let me get my driver's keys. We are not going to be here long. We will be taking you to the main Beijing Police Station, where you will be debriefed. The Canadian Embassy will send a senior official to meet you there as well." Henry said, quite concerned at the look on my face.

He headed back inside the station and came back with a bunch of car keys. He took me over to the car we came in and put me in the back seat. He then told me that he would be back in about 10 minutes, but would I feel better if he locked the doors.

I said, "Please lock the doors and don't take too long. I am getting paranoid sitting here by myself."

Henry looked at me and said gently, "I know how you must be feeling. This bad situation is now over. You are on your way home in a few hours. Just a debrief at the main station and then home."

Chapter 18

Beijing Main Police Station, Friday night

We arrived at the Beijing main police station at just past 9.00 pm by the clock in the entrance hall. Henry shook my hand and said, "You are in good hands now." I shook his hand and hugged the man. I felt a real sense of relief for the first time in a week. I couldn't tell you how good this felt. Almost like a rebirth. A sense of wellbeing and almost giddy to be alive and free.

Henry handed me off to another uniformed officer who escorted me to the fifth floor. He showed me into a large conference room with a huge table and about 20 chairs. He asked me if I needed anything. I said a bottle of water. He brought it and left me.

I was alone in this conference room for almost an hour. I had seen no one since the bottle of water was brought to me. I began to worry again. The place was very quiet, and I looked out the interior window at the corridor that ran around the entire fifth floor. The center of the building was open from the ground up to what looked like the sixth floor. I could see the roof from the window in the conference room.

Then I see a uniformed office walk out of another room across the open area on the opposite side and I waved at him. He walked around the end of the corridor and came into the conference room. In very bad English, asked me what I needed.

"I need to talk to someone about debriefing me," I said. He did not understand what I was saying. I tried to indicate that I needed to speak with someone. Eventually after a few tries, he seemed to get the message. He said to wait. He headed back over to the corridor on the other side and disappeared through a doorway. I waited another 10 minutes and figured he had forgotten all about me.

After what seemed like half-an-hour, a different guy came out of the same doorway, around the walkway, and into the conference room. I was totally frustrated by this time. He apologized for the long wait.

He told me his name. I immediately forgot it. He said, "Sorry you had to wait so long for me. Not too many of our detectives speak good enough English to handle your debriefing."

"Also, I needed to be present for the initial booking of the kidnappers and hear some details of who they were and any other information on any other persons associated with the kidnapping. You told one of our special team operatives there were more than the three people we picked up," he said.

"Yes, there were actually five in total. Four men and one woman. I told this to Henry, who was in charge of the rescue team. He was not aware of any others involved in the kidnapping."

The detective said, "Yes I understand this. When the detectives who did the initial interrogation, they did not give up anyone else. They kept saying it was just the three of them. Albert Ho who we think is the ringleader, was in fact the only person who said anything. The other two were in separate interrogations but refused to speak with the detectives."

"Wait a minute," I said "You mean they are all in this same building?"

"Yes, this is the main Beijing Police Station. They are being held in the ground floor holding area and all in separate interrogating rooms." This might take some time as we need to corroborate some information between their story and yours."

"Why is that necessary", I said.

"There are several important reasons. The most important is why they kidnapped you, a foreigner, and if they injured you in any way. This will be a major factor in what they were charged with and could be a very serious charge, possibly resulting in the death penalty," the detective said.

He then asked me for my version of events of the kidnapping. I went over everything I could remember from last Friday morning when the young woman came into my office to Sunday evening when the actual kidnapping took place. Then the time from late Sunday night until I was rescued earlier that Friday evening by Henry and his special team. He listened quietly for the most part. Only asking a few questions for clarification. Once I told him that was my story, he said "You have been through quite the ordeal."

Then he said, "I need you to be patient as I have to get back downstairs for possibly another hour to determine what the charges will be before I can get back up here. Is there anything else you need?"

I asked, "Is there a phone I can use. I need to make a few important phone calls."

The detective said, "The first phone call you need to make is to the Foreign Affairs Office in Ottawa. They are standing by to hear from you and have been calling both the Beijing Embassy and here at the Police Station, in an effort to talk to you." Anyone else you need to call, please do that after you talk to Canada."

"Okay, is there a phone I can use." I asked him.

"We have an international phone set-up in our communication center near my office on the other side. Please come with me and I'll have one of my operators connect you with the Canadian Foreign Office in Ottawa."

We cross over to the other side of the building. As we walk around, I noticed that there were several offices on this side of the open space, and all seem to be administrative in nature. Glass windows allow a view into these offices which were next to each other right around the entire section across from the conference room. They all appeared to be single occupant type cubicles facing into a central core area.

We went in the same door the detective came out of and down a short interior corridor. We then turned right and entered another office. We were now in a smaller room that has quite a few phones and some other audio equipment on a long desk along one wall. One man sat at this desk with headphones. Then in the center of the room, there was a square table with four chairs and an old-style black telephone. It did not have a dial pad or buttons to select phone numbers. He asked me to sit in one of the chairs, and he sat in another.

The detective then called out to the operator and asked him to connect to Ottawa, Canada. The man nodded his head and started punching some buttons on his phone. We sat silently for a few minutes. Then the black phone on the desk rings. The detective told me to pick up.

"Hello," I said.

"Hello. Is this Mr. Dave Rohee? The voice on the phone said to me.

"Yes, it is. Who is this?"

"This is Sargent Rollins of the Canadian Foreign Affairs RCMP detachment. I am talking to you from Ottawa. Where are you now?" He asked.

I told him I'm at the main Beijing main Police Station. He asked if I was safe and unharmed. I told him yes, I'm ok.

"I am very pleased that you have been rescued. We here at the Foreign Affairs office have been worried about you. Glad to hear that you are in good hands."

Sargent Rollins said, "I now have to let the Canadian Embassy in Beijing know that you are safe and your present location. The Embassy will be sending a senior official to meet with you very shortly. Please let me speak to the Police officer that is with you."

I passed the phone over to the detective, and they have a conversation for a few minutes. Then the detective says, "Yes, its perfectly safe for Mr. Rohee here in the Station, and we will wait until the Embassy official arrives." He then hung up the phone.

He took me back over to the conference room to wait. Before he left, I asked if I can make another call. He asked if it was a local call, and I told him yes. He said I could use his cell phone.

It was now almost ten o'clock on Friday night. I called my Chief Instructor and assistant manager Brian. He picked up and said, "Hello? Who is this?"

When I tell him who it was, he freaked out! "Dave? Where are you? Are you all right? What's going on mate?" His Australian heritage came on strong.

I told him where I was and, he said, "Tell whoever you are with that I am coming to see you now." I know where the Main Beijing Police

Station is. I will be there in twenty minutes. Really happy to hear your voice! See you in a few. Don't move an inch." Brian said.

I gave the detective back his cell phone, and he tapped me on the shoulder and said, "I will be back as soon as possible. You will soon have visitors, I assume." He left me alone again in the conference room.

Chapter 19

Beijing Main Police Station,
Friday night
The Reunion

I sat back down at the conference room table and anxiously waited to see who would show up next.

I was so happy to see my big blustery Australian Chief Instructor Brian! He had big feet, and I could hear him a long way away. He came into the conference room like the wind and grabbed me up in a bear hug. Almost literally. Brian was well over six feet and could play Aussie Rules football. He had craggy features but a winning smile and was a genuinely nice guy. He had lots of patience with our new students and had managed to charm most of them to sign up for our technical English training classes. Great guy to have as an assistant manager. His wife worked in the Australian Embassy in Beijing, so he had many good connections to help our organization with contacts in the Chinese administration.

I am so happy to see the big guy, tears began to fall, and I couldn't seem to stop them. He said, "Go ahead and get it all out, mate. You need to decompress. Let it all hang out.'"

I cried some more and then started to answer some of his questions. We talked about Albert who he had met and said, "I never liked the guy, Dave. I know you and he were introduced through a friend, but I never liked him and thought he was a snake in the grass. Well, he has proven the type of snake he is. I hope they lock his ass up and throw away the key!" Brian said.

We talked some more about the office and what had happened during the week. We talked about Baby Face coming into the office and conning Olivia and getting my passport, money, and files. He told me not to be too hard on Olivia. She had no idea about the passport or international travel requirements for Canadians.

I agreed with him. "Olivia is my right hand, and I could never replace her. I trust her with my life and very nearly did." I explained what Albert had proposed to get into the company bank accounts and clean us out.

Brian started laughing like a hyena! "I would have paid money to see that routine," he said. "I can't believe they actually thought that was going to work. What a bunch of idiots."

We talked some more. Then we heard footsteps out in the corridor. It sounded like a few people. Then a police officer in uniform stepped into the room, and behind him was a woman who was dressed up and looked like an official. And that she is. She introduced herself as a Senior Official from the Canadian Embassy. Her name was Sheila Stepard-Johnson.

She asked if I was ok. Very official and not very friendly at first. When I told her that I was as well as could be expected, she thawed a little. She said, "We have never had a situation like this where a Canadian citizen has been kidnapped here in China. And certainly, the first time I have ever had to deal with this type of problem."

I told her it was also the first time I had been kidnapped and certainly had no desire to have that type of experience ever again in this lifetime.

She smiled briefly at my comment. "I'm sure you won't."

"Have the Beijing Police debriefed you as yet?" She asked me.

"Yes, but I'm not sure it is complete. There is some discrepancy between my version of events and the three kidnappers they caught." I said.

"What is the difference," she asked.

"There were actually five kidnappers," I said. "Four men and one woman. But the three kidnappers they caught were saying it's only the three of them."

"Well, the police will get to the bottom of that problem, I'm sure. What would you like to do now? Would you like to go home?"

"Home where?" I asked. "They broke into my apartment and stole a bunch of stuff, my computer, cameras, and God knows what else. I would not feel safe there ever again. Plus, they haven't caught all the kidnappers, so I am very concerned for my safety." I blurted out anxiously.

"Well," Stepard-Johnson said, The Embassy does not have a budget to pay for a hotel or security for you to stay for any length of time, so I'm not sure what other option we have."

At this point, Brian jumped in and said, "Never mind, Dave will be staying with me until we can find him a new place to stay."

The Embassy official did not like the way the conversation was heading, and I could see from her demeanor that she was uncomfortable with Brian's comment.

At this time, I have had enough to deal with over the past week and told Stepard-Johnson what I thought.

"I really appreciate everything the Embassy and you have done. However, I am still very concerned about my personal safety. I have a company to run and not sure what my next steps were likely to be for the immediate future. I will be accepting Brian's offer to stay with him, at least until we can figure out where I will be living." I said, trying to pacify the moment.

Brian said, "Dave let's get out of here. I'm sure you need a good night's rest and get away from all this craziness. You smell like a sewer, mate. You need a bath to get yourself cleaned up. My wife is not going to want you with that kind of odor in our apartment."

"This is what five days of no showers or shaving will do for you. I'm not sure I can leave until the detective gets back. He went back to talk with the interrogation officers and may have some more follow-up questions." I said.

"Ok, I'm going to go down to the first floor and ask for him. What's his name?" Brian asked.

"I actually can't remember. He told me, but I immediately forgot his name. The only name I remember is Henry, the Special Operative's name that rescued me with his team. I don't remember much else. My brain is fried." I said.

Brian shouldered his way out the glass door of the conference room, and his heavy footsteps receded down the corridor to the elevator.

When he left, the Embassy lady said, "Are you sure this is what you want to do. How well do you know this person?"

"He is my Assistant Manager and Chief Instructor for my company. I trust him. He and I have a lot in common, and his wife also works at the Australian Embassy here in Beijing."

"What about going back to Canada. Is that not a better plan?" she asked.

"No. I have a new aviation business that I am setting up here in China and need to stay and get it up and running. I am not going to let a gang of thugs ruin my life or my work. I am staying, and that's final."

"If that's your choice, then so be it. The Embassy can only recommend certain choices and options for Canadian citizens living in foreign countries. We are responsible for their overall safety. More than that is outside our purview." She said.

"I appreciate that more than you know. I have been in close contact with the Transportation Group at the Embassy on a regular basis. They have been incredibly helpful in guiding me to the right contacts with the regional airlines in many provinces and going so far as setting up introductory meetings with a few CEO's. In case you were not aware, I have been invited to quite a few Embassy functions for a meet and greet with government officials and aviation contacts. After one of these parties, an article about my contract with a Chinese Aviation University made the front page of a Chinese newspaper."

"Unfortunately, that article is the reason for my kidnapping. The ringleader saw the article and was pissed at me. He always wanted to be my partner, but he turned out to be nothing but a con man and a thief. He told me during the kidnapping that he was going to get me thrown out of China and my visa revoked. He is an angry son-of-a-bitch and trying to steal my business." I said.

"What! You know these people who kidnapped you?" She asked.

"I only know the ringleader. He obviously recruited the others to make sure the kidnapping went off as planned, and they were supposed to get away with five hundred thousand US dollars ransom. However, they were a bunch of idiots or amateurs and never really had a hope of getting any money. I am not worth that kind of money to anyone who might be willing to pay a ransom for me."

"I am lucky to be alive today and free. Thanks to the Chinese special operations team. They saved my bacon today!" I didn't add that I cried like a baby when they rescued me. That, I would keep to myself.

"I met the ringleader in Vancouver a couple of years ago and feel he may even be a Canadian resident. Apparently, his father was a governor for a large province in China but has retired to Canada. I will have to check on his status."

The Embassy Official said, "You should do that. If he is a Canadian resident or citizen, the Attorney General can hold him criminally liable and prosecute him for this offense."

"I never thought that would be even feasible. This kidnapping happened in China, not Canada." I said.

"Doesn't matter," she said. If he is legally a Canadian, then he can be prosecuted anyway. It does not matter where this event occurred, that is a factor. It was a Canadian perpetrating a crime against another Canadian! He would need to be extradited to Canada to face the charges. We have a reciprocal extradition agreement with China."

Just then, we hear footsteps coming along the corridor. Brian comes in with the detective. The detective says, "Your friend is a very persuasive person. He says he needs to take you home. He says you need a safe place to recuperate, and I agree."

"It is okay for you to leave now. We will need you to be available for further interviews or assistance in the criminal proceedings. You will most likely be contacted by the Provincial Prosecutor for more details. You will also be called as the main witness, so please do not leave town or the country without letting them know. I'm sure they will be in touch in the next few weeks once the criminal case is being investigated. Again, my apologies for the way you have been treated by these criminals, but rest assured that they will be given just punishment."

I thanked him for his help and shook his hand. I get up to leave and grab the camera and travel bags with me. I shake the Embassy official's hand, and we headed out into the corridor.

The detective led us to the elevator and accompanied us to the ground floor. Brian told the detective his car was in front of the Station. We left by the front entrance. There were a lot of uniformed policemen, standing around and looking at us as we left.

The Embassy official heads out away from us and said goodbye as she left. We crossed the street and got into Brian's car. I immediately started to shake. I felt I was having a nervous breakdown. I put my head back on the headrest and took a few deep breaths. Brian asked if I am all right. I took a few moments before I answered.

"Mate, thank God for you. Only now do I really feel free! I can't tell you how happy I am that you are here. And thanks for doing what you did in there for me. Not sure how I would have been able to cope with much more tonight."

"That's why I got you out of there. I know you need some time to get your head around the events of this past week. You need some quiet time. We can sort out the other bullshit later. Let's get you home, cleaned up, and in bed. My wife keeps a clean smelling home, and my young daughter would tell you exactly how bad you smell."

I am teary-eyed at the thought of spending the rest of this night as a free person. The nightmares of the past several nights will probably haunt me for years to come. We drove for another few minutes, and I tried to calm my mind and rest my thoughts.

All of a sudden, I realized that I had not called Teresita! Because I did not have my cell phone, I was only concerned about my safety and was worried that two kidnappers were still on the loose.

"Brian, I need to call Teresita. She needs to know that I have been rescued and that I am ok. Could I use your cell phone?"

"Of course, mate. Do you want to call her right now?"

He hands me his phone, and I dial our home number in Coquitlam. The connection takes a minute or so, and I am already nervous. The phone connects and starts ringing.

"Hello? Who is this?" Teresita asks.

"It's me, Teresita. I am free!" I am crying as I say this. I can't seem to stop the crying jag.

"Oh my God, Dave. I'm so happy to hear your voice. We only heard the news that you were rescued a couple of hours ago. I was hoping to hear your voice. Are you ok?" Teresita cried joyfully.

"How did you know I was rescued?" I asked.

"We heard from the RCMP office in Ottawa. You have no idea how many people have been working to catch the kidnappers. We've actually had two detectives in our home since Monday. We have all sorts of recording equipment on the dining table, and they have been recording all the conversations I have had with the kidnappers. The RCMP and Interpol have been coordinating their efforts with the Chinese Secret Police to try and figure out where you were and who had kidnapped you." Teresita says.

"Do you know who kidnapped you? She said.

"Yes, I do, and so do you. You are not going to believe this. Remember the Chinese guy who Lydia said was someone she knew and wanted an introduction to the Film Institute in Vancouver? Well, that is the son-of-a-bitch that kidnapped me. He and four others!" I angrily almost shout the words.

"You're kidding me," she said. "Why would he do something like that?"

"That's a long story, my love. And for another day. Right now, I am in Brian's car, and we are heading to his place. I will be staying with him until we decide what to do next." I'm still shaking and very nervous." I said, "I'll call you tomorrow."

"I'm so happy you are ok! I hope you will come home soon." Teresita said.

"That may be a bit of a problem," I said. "They stole a lot of stuff, including my passport, and I have to get that sorted out first. And I have to make a decision on what to do about the business before I can leave."

"Yes, I knew it would not be that simple. Please take care of yourself and get home in one piece."

"Teresita, from what little I have heard so far from the Beijing Police, you may have saved my life. Apparently, the Chinese Secret Police were taping the phone calls between the kidnappers and Canada, and when you hung up on them, and they called back, the police were able to identify the approximate location where I was being held. I owe you my life. I mean it." Tears started rolling down my cheeks.

"I'll talk to you tomorrow, my love. Good night. Thanks for looking out for me."

She said goodbye softly, and I realize that she was also crying. I closed the phone and handed the phone back to Brian.

"Everything okay there, mate?" Brian asked.

"Just glad to be free, Brian. Still having a tough time processing the facts. How I got mixed up with these goons in the first place and needed my head examined."

"Well, let's get you some much-needed rest, and then we'll talk about the future."

I put my head back against the headrest, closed my eyes, and tried to forget the past five days!

CHAPTER 20

Beijing
The Aftermath

Brian and his wife June, were up early. I was sleeping on the couch in the living room. I managed to open my eyes and tell them good morning. Brian said that breakfast would be served in a few minutes and asked if I wanted anything special. I told him that anything right now would be special. He smiled and headed into the kitchen to join his wife. I heard lots of activity and soft conversation. I knew they were talking about me.

I used the bathroom, actually brush my teeth, and almost felt human again. When we came in late last night, I did not pay much attention to Brian's apartment. He ran a bath, and I had carefully lowered myself into the tub and luxuriated until the water got cold. I think I remembered drying myself and sitting on the couch. That was the last thing I remembered. This morning there was a pillow under my head and a blanket covering me. When did this happen? I wondered.

Brian's daughter came out of her bedroom and looked at me. "Hello," I said. What's your name? She smiled and said her name is Mary. I'm six, she said. She looks just like her mother.

"Breakfast is ready," Brian said. We sat at the table and dug in. Mary keeps looking at me.

"I can't tell you how good this feels," I told them and thanked them again for everything.

After we had breakfast, Brian asked me what I would like to do. He promised to call Olivia if he had heard anything but had not called her as yet. I told him to call her now. He called her, and I can almost hear her voice over the phone. They talked for a few minutes. He said yes, "Dave is here, and he's okay."

"She wants to talk to you." Brian handed me the phone.

"Hi, Olivia. How are you?" I asked.

"Dave, I am so glad to hear your voice. I have been so worried about you all week. I messed up when the guy came to pick up your passport, money, and some files. I think I knew something was wrong. Anyway, Brian went to the Embassy, and that's when we knew you were kidnapped. Are you sure you are ok? How did this happen?"

"You are definitely not going to believe who did this. It was Albert! Remember how mad he was when we decided not to do any more business with him. Well, he decided to get back at me. When the Embassy had that big cocktail party, and we made the papers with the deal with the Civil Aviation University of China, he was really mad."

"He was the one who sent that young lady to our office last Friday to set me up. And I fell for it. Hook, line, and sinker! Anyway, my dear, I am happy to be free and even happier to be talking to you. I will be staying with Brian until we figure out where I will move to next. They were able to get into my apartment and steal a bunch of stuff. My computer, cameras, my computer travel bag, laptop and God only knows what else. I'm not going back there without some security guards."

"Are you going into the office today," Olivia asked.

I looked over at Brian and asked him if he had any plans for today. He shook his head.

I told Olivia that Brian would give me a ride over to the office in about an hour. I just wanted to check my office and see what they had taken and if I need to report anything else to the local Police.

"I will see you there, Dave, I can't wait to see you." Just so you know, now that have caught Albert I'm sure they are going to throw the book at him. Did they hurt you? Olivia asked.

"No, thank God for small mercies," I said. "See you in a while." I shut the phone off and handed it back to Brian.

After we had breakfast, Brian's wife took away the dishes and told Brian to take me into the office. She and Mary will be okay for the rest of the morning doing girl things.

I asked if they minded if I took a shower. They both looked at me like I was crazy. I said I hadn't felt clean for over a week. They said to go ahead. I did and felt like a new person. I still had to put on the same old dirty clothes but no underwear. Sometime today, I would have to get to a store and buy some replacements until we could visit my apartment. I'm not going there anytime soon.

I'm still concerned that the other two kidnappers had not been caught. By now, they should have all been taken into custody. I wonder why Albert and the other two did not give up the woman and the Major.

We headed over to the office around 10.30 am. I got into my office, and nothing seems out of place. Until I opened my top drawer and saw that my folder where I keep my passport, travel currency, and key to my apartment were missing. They took all the emergency stash I had in the folder Three different currencies. US dollars, Hong Kong Dollars, and Chinese Yuan. I was really pissed. Brian looked on quietly.

I heard the main office door open and small footsteps hurrying along the corridor. I look up and see Olivia's smiling face. I move out from behind my desk, and we hug for quite a few minutes. She started crying, and so do I. This is getting to be a regular thing with me. My emotions were pretty raw at the moment, so I didn't really care.

After we're through with the waterworks, the three of us sit down at the conference room table and talk about all the events leading up to last week's kidnapping. We went over the young woman coming into the office and waiting for me to arrive from Hong Kong. Olivia said she would not tell anyone why she was there, other than she had spoken with me, and I had agreed to meet with her on Friday. Then we had a short meeting when I returned to the office. I told Olivia and Brian that she wanted to talk about becoming a pilot. Her English was not bad, and we agreed to meet again on the following Monday for a student pilot interview with Brian.

I knew now that was a lie. She and I never spoke. Friday was the first time I met her, and I never spoke to her prior to Friday.

Then I told Brian and Olivia what happened that weekend. I was in the apartment doing some research on Chinese airlines and putting together a powerpoint presentation for Jennifer to translate into Mandarin.

I told them here is what happened....

Saturday morning
Prior to the Kidnapping on Sunday afternoon

I was sitting at my desk in the apartment. My cell phone rang. The voice on the phone says, "Mr. Rohee, I apologize for the phone call. My name is Yvonne. We met at your office yesterday. Do you remember me?"

"I do. We set up a meeting for next Monday for you to come into the office for an interview with my Chief Instructor." I said.

"I know we did. My family is very afraid for me. They think that flying is a dangerous career, especially for a female. They have asked me to invite you to dinner so they can meet you. They are nice people but older and know very little about aviation. They want to ask you some questions about your program, and I hope you would not mind doing this for me." She said.

During our initial advertising with the various universities, there have been many times parents showed up with their teenage children to listen to our presentations and ask questions. This is the first time any company, local or foreign had ever started a flight training program outside of the Chinese government. The government had one major aviation university in a western province, but can only produce a small number of qualified pilots every year. China needs many more aviation and flight training programs to expand the airline industry, especially with the prospect of hosting the 2008 Olympic games.

I thought about this for a short time. I couldn't see any downside to this request and felt that since dinner is also included, and I have to eat, so why not. I agreed to her invitation. So when are we talking about, I asked.

"We will have a car pick you up at 5.30 pm on Sunday. We can have dinner and spend some time trying to convince my parents to join your flight training program." Yvonne said.

"Okay," I said. "That works for me." I put this out of my mind and concentrated on my research. Many hours later, I got up and had a stretch. Then I headed down to the basement in the adjoining recreation center for a swim. After the workout, I headed back up to the apartment and cooked up a small dinner for myself. I watched some English television and then hit the sack.

Sunday afternoon
Prior to The Kidnapping

The phone rang at 4.50 pm. When I answered the phone. It is Yvonne. She said they would have the car downstairs at 5.30 pm. Her parents would meet us at the restaurant. Would I mind coming downstairs and meeting her and the driver. That would save some time, she said.

Not thinking about personal safety, I forgot that all visitors to our two buildings where foreigners were allowed to live have to announce who they are going to visit and get a pass that has to be signed by the resident. This did not bother me in the least. An error I would soon regret.

I finish getting dressed and headed to the elevator. I am on the 23rd floor, and the elevator takes only a few seconds to make it to the ground floor. As I walked out to the entryway, I noticed the guardhouse had one guard inside. The bar is down, and I walked around to one side. I looked out at the street and then saw someone waving at me. I saw a white car on the opposite side of the road and slightly past our entrance. I recognized Yvonne, and she beckons me over to that side of the road.

I do not notice that she is standing in front of the license plate and covering my view of the numbers. Another error I made in assuming that all was well.

She opened the back door to the car, and I got in. She then introduced the driver, whose name I don't remember, probably a Chinese name. She apologized for the small car and said her family had used their family car to go directly to the restaurant. I did not react to this news either.

Then I told Olivia and Brian the horrifying events and the rest of the ride, the actual kidnapping, and the events of the week in great detail. I told them about the plan to have Olivia go to the bank on Saturday (that would have been today!!!) and withdraw all the money from the two GIT bank accounts.

Brian started laughing again like a hyena! He couldn't stop. He asked me how they were going to get Olivia to do that. I told him that they were possibly going to kidnap her Friday night at her home and forced her to go to the bank on Saturday. They both have a horrified look on their faces. Olivia started crying. I tried to explain that this was only a plan that Albert thought up at a moment's notice when it looked as if Teresita was not going to pay the ransom. I told her that I didn't think they were going to go through with that plan.

Brian said, "These have got to be the stupidest bunch of assholes I have ever heard of! Forcing Olivia to go into a bank with all that security and to withdraw money. They have got to be mentally deranged."

"You know what, Dave, I think you were kidnapped by the VID gang."

"What the heck is VID Brian?" I asked him.

"It stands for **V**ictims of the **I**ncredibly **D**umb!" He laughed.

Olivia quietened down after Brian told me this joke. We talked about this situation some more and then headed down to the restaurant in the building next door to have something to eat. When we were finished, I asked Olivia if she had any Yuan in the office safe. She said she did. I tell her that I needed to get some new clothes and underwear. We went back to the office and she got me what I needed.

I told them to give me a few minutes as I needed to call Teresita. Olivia said to say hello for her, and I went into my office and called Canada.

Teresita answers the phone, and we talk about lots of small stuff. She said she had called the airline and put in her name for the next Beijing flight. She said she should be able to see me by late next week and will stay for at least five days. Due to her seniority, she has lots of discretionary time to work with and time off as well. I was also sure the airline would give her whatever time she needed.

Teresita said the RCMP officers had packed up all the equipment and left our home as soon as they got the news from Ottawa that I was safe. One of the detectives told her that we would both need to be debriefed by both the RCMP and the local Coquitlam police once I got back to Canada.

Then we talk for a few minutes about the following week and finding a new place for me to stay. Olivia headed home, and Brian and I go shopping for two hours, and then both headed back to his place.

The rest of the weekend passed uneventfully. I relaxed and enjoyed finishing the book "Hostage" that I was reading during my kidnapping episode. Brian had a hard time believing that was the book I had in my travel bag. I showed him the book, and we have a quiet laugh between us. The VID gang indeed.

Epilogue

The first week after the kidnapping was an underwhelming time for me. Nothing seemed as urgent or important enough for me to get excited. I had no passport to travel even back home to Canada. That would have to wait. Teresita would be here in three days, and I can't wait to see her.

On Monday, Olivia spoke to the building manager, and I was able to rent a suite on the seventh floor. Our office was on the second. It seemed appropriate that I would be close to the office and still feel safe. We told no one where I would be living.

Late Monday, one of our other English instructors accompanied Brian and me to my old apartment and helped me to pack up some essential items and clothes and moved me to the new apartment on the seventh floor in our office building. It is a multi-use rental building with residential suites above the fifth floor. Really handy and very private, especially due to my recent situation.

Wednesday morning we got a call from the RCMP detachment at the Canadian Embassy. They requested me to come down to the Embassy for an interview and debriefing session. I asked if it could be later in the week and they said no. It needed to be today. So Brian and I made arrangements to meet at the Embassy after lunch.

When we arrived at the Embassy, we went through the usual security protocol to enter the hallowed area that Canada enjoys in any foreign country where it has an Embassy. When we were directed to a conference room, there were two RCMP officers already in the room with a bunch of paperwork on the table.

They introduced themselves as Sargent Davidson and Corporal O'Ryan. When we went to sit down, the Sargent asked Brian to wait outside. Brian was not happy and let them know it. "What is this, he asked. Why can't I stay?"

Sargent Davidson tells him it's a personal interview with a Canadian citizen who has been the victim of a kidnapping. They asked him politely to leave, and he patted me on the shoulder and said, "Mate, I will be right outside."

When the interview started, it sounded more like an interrogation. They fired questions back and forth at me. I responded as best I could. The initial questioning was surrounding Albert and how we met and our business relationship that went sour! I went through the entire sad story about our meeting in Canada, and subsequent falling out in China. At first, they did not seem too impressed with my side of the events. That is until we got to the kidnapping event. Then the tone of the interview changed.

Then I learned some interesting things about the actual time I was incarcerated by the kidnappers. When the phone calls were made to Canada and Albert was changing out the SIM cards in his phone, that alerted the Chinese cyber-crime unit that something was amiss in a location south of Beijing.

Since the Chinese Secret Police were already informed that a Canadian had been kidnapped, they were on the alert for any suspicious phone calls, especially international calls. And many calls made from one location with different SIM cards immediately got their attention.

Chinese law enforcement had complete control over almost everything in China, and this was just one area where they excel. In addition to the international calls, there were several calls from a local number to the same location from where the international calls originated.

I now learned from the RCMP that Baby Face was on parole from a violent crime that he had been convicted for, and his phone was being monitored and recorded by the police. Apparently, his wife kept calling his cell phone, asking him where he was and why he had not come home for days.

With these pieces of information, the Chinese Secret Police knew the location of Baby Face by late Tuesday night! They did not know that this was where I was being held until Interpol requested information on an address south of Beijing. Once the RCMP, Interpol, and the Chinese police were connected and looking at the same data, they were able to determine the exact location and the suspected identity of some of the kidnappers.

The three agencies had agreed to wait until some type of surveillance was put in place by the Secret Police before any decision was made to intervene.

This all changed on Thursday when they learned from the recorded phone calls that if the kidnappers did not get the money by Saturday they were going to kill me, the Chinese Secret Police decided that they had to act on Friday.

And that is how the Special Operations team was assembled, and the rescue was planned and executed early Friday evening. Flawlessly as it turned out for me.

Near the end of the interview, I asked what was going to happen about the other two kidnappers. The young woman and the fourth man (the Major). The Sargent said that nowhere in the investigation or notes that they had in front of them were the other two kidnappers mentioned at any time.

Then they asked me to meet with the Embassy Official, who came to the Beijing Police Station on Friday night. They said she had some more information for me. I asked if it was possible to see her while I was here at the Embassy. They checked and said she was willing to see me now.

We shook hands, and they wished me good luck with my China business project. Then Brian and I went over to a second Embassy annex, and I waited to see Ms. Stepard-Johnson. When I was asked to come into her office, I was surprised to see something I had not expected to see again.

My computer bag was sitting on one of her office chairs. What a shock that was! She asked me to sit down. I grabbed a chair opposite her desk and looked at the bag sitting on the chair next to me. We looked at each other and then she asked me if I was okay. I said, "For the most part, yes."

"Please tell me what this is about," I said, looking at the bag.

"In a minute." I need to tell you how I came to have it and what this means."

I was quite upset at this, and said, "Please tell me now!"

She then told me, "A Chinese woman came into the Embassy two days ago and asked to see me. She introduced herself as Albert's wife. She said he was not part of the kidnapping and that anything that I said about Albert was a lie. Then she said that this bag was left by you in their apartment some time ago, and she wanted to make sure it was returned to you. Please check inside and let me know if you recognize anything."

By the time she was finished, I was truly pissed. "I can't believe this. And it sounds to me like you believe this?" I said.

She said, "Mr. Rohee, I don't know what to believe. Apparently, this woman is a very real celebrity here in China. She is an accomplished ballerina and has quite a following."

"I don't care what she is or who she knows. Everything she told you is a lie. I went to their apartment once when I first came to China years ago and long before Albert, and I severed our relationship. I never took my computer bag there. I only used it when I traveled. My laptop and personal documents were all in here, and these I used on a daily basis, either at home or in my office. They obviously stole these items and the bag when they ransacked my apartment after they had kidnapped me," I told her.

She looked a little shocked at my vehement remarks. She said, "Mr. Rohee, please calm down. I had already told the RCMP officers you met with earlier, and they also think the woman has to be lying. I am just relating to you the story she told me."

I went through the computer bag and felt that most of the stuff that was important is all there. I got up and told Ms. Stepard-Johnson, I was leaving. Could I please take my bag? She said to go ahead and take it.

I left her office and met Brian in the waiting area. He looked at me and knew I was angry, so he did not say anything. We went through the ritual of exiting the Embassy security and headed back to the office. Brian got off at the office floor. I bypassed the office floor and headed up to my apartment on the seventh. When I got in, I threw myself on the couch and tried to calm down. I also tried to meditate as this is the only thing that sometimes allowed me to ease my stress level and bring me back to some level of normal behavior. Olivia called my cell phone and asked if I was okay. Brian told her that I was upset. I told her to close up the office. I would not be coming back down to the office today.

The next complicated issue was to have a new passport issued so I could travel. This was another bureaucratic nightmare. Even though the Embassy knew the full story about the kidnapping, proper protocol had to be followed. In any foreign country where a Canadian passport is stolen or lost, a Police report had to be submitted to the Embassy, in order for them to issue a new passport.

This now takes on the semblance of a three-ring circus in the local police station where Brian and I were forced to go and file a police report! Of course, very few people in the police station spoke English, so we were forced to wait an interminable time for a translation to be made of the report. Then we had to deal with the fact that because they were not aware of the kidnapping event, we got pushback at every sentence and as if we were lying! This process really busted my balls! It was a good thing Brian was there with me to keep me from committing some grievous error and shouting at these officers.

Finally, we got the document we needed, both in English and Chinese. We left the station after almost two hours of wasted time. We headed to the Canadian Embassy and filled out the documents required for a new passport to be issued. They said it would take two days to complete the required paperwork. They asked if I wanted an emergency travel permit, but I said two days was fine.

A really strange event occurred the next morning. I was still upstairs in my apartment when Olivia called me. She said you are not going to believe this.

"A lawyer showed up a little while ago and asked for you. Brian took him into your office and asked him why he was here. He said that he is here on instructions from his client Albert Ho. Albert is asking you to drop the kidnapping charges as it was a misunderstanding!" Olivia said in an angry tone of voice. "Can you believe this crap?"

I said, "What did Brian tell him."

"Brian told him he should contact the Crown Prosecutor. He said we had no say in what the state charges were, and we do not want to interfere with the court's process. Then apparently, Brian asked him not very politely to leave. I think his words were, don't let the door hit you in the ass!"

The rest of the story was all about trying to revive my aviation business and trying to get my life back in some form of order. Teresita gave her grudging consent for me not to return to Canada and to try and complete the project I originally started.

I decided to stay the course and acquire the Flight School permit, that was my initial project. After suffering through many bureaucratic hassles and endless delays, I was issued the first, and probably only foreign-owned Flight School permit to operate in China. However, the forces were against me from actually starting the school. The Chinese government probably realized that allowing a foreign company to operate a Flight School in China would not be a good idea. Many obstacles were strewn in my path, and eventually, I was forced to throw in the towel.

Then the nightmares began to get worse. I found myself suddenly waking up in a fright and sweating bullets! I couldn't function as I had previous to the kidnapping and eventually, Olivia suggested that I get some medical help. I called Peter at the Embassy, and he said the best place he could recommend would be the American Diplomatic Hospital in north Beijing.

He said he knew them from previous medical emergencies that occurred in China with a few Canadians, and they would certainly be willing to help. He made a call and set it up for me.

When the office staff was trying to teach me Mandarin, they made up 3x5 cards for me to take whenever I went out on my own. This was a godsend for me. Olivia wrote English on one side and Mandarin on the other. If I could not pronounce it properly, I would just show the Chinese translation to the taxi driver. It worked very well! After a few months of tutoring from the three ladies in the office at lunchtime, I was able to venture out on my own, both on the subway and the local taxis with basic Chinese words and a couple of phrases. But now I was feeling less safe and secure and not wanting to be out on my own.

Olivia made the first appointment for me. She asked if I needed her to come with me. I said yes. We went to the US Diplomatic Hospital and met with a Doctor. Once he heard the problem, I was referred to a female Therapist who was working with Vietnam vets who had suffered serious head and brain injuries from severe trauma, now called PTSD.

When I met her the first time, she said she was having a lot of success with a treatment called EMDR – **E**ye **M**ovement **D**esensitization and **R**eprocessing, and would I be willing to try it. I said I would. Then she told me that she needed to talk to my lawyer about the upcoming court case. When I asked why, she said because when the treatment was completed, I would probably forget a lot of the details of the event! I was somewhat shocked at this and told her my reaction.

"I have been a pilot for over thirty years. I am a flight instructor and trainer. I very much doubt that I will ever forget anything that happened during those five days. I remembered every single detail of every single hour of the days I was held captive. My memory is probably the best and worst part of my psyche. My nightmares are very vivid and in living color!" I said.

I don't remember her name, but her advice was quite unique and refreshing. She said the treatment would probably last at least four or more sessions of 90 minutes each. And she would assess the success of the treatment as we went along. She also said that I had to choose a color that represented the event and another color that represented a safe place. She applied a few electrodes to my temples and forehead.

Then I was told to think of the color that represented danger (I chose red) and one that represented the safe place (I chose blue). Once the electrical impulses started, I could feel my eyes fluttering in time to the impulses. At the end of each session, the impulses were gradually slowed down and stopped. Then, she would ask what color was most predominant at the end of the session.

And lo and behold, by the end of the third session, I was starting to feel less stressed out, and the nightmares had receded to only a few times a week. The EMDR program was really working.

When I completed my fourth session, the doctor said she felt that I was at a point where I did not need any further treatments. And asked me how did I feel. She also asked what I would do now that the treatment was completed. I told her I would like to write a book about my experiences and hope that no one would ever have to suffer something like a kidnapping! She and I were both emotional at the end. I gave her a hug, and she wished me good luck with my business and the book. This is that book!

Final words

After the investigation was completed the court case was finally scheduled. Both Teresita and Olivia were by my side in the courtroom. There were some tense moments during the trial. Two of them are worth mentioning here. The first was the case for the defense. Their argument was that it was not a kidnapping. It was a case of a business meeting that went bad and lasted for five days!

The second was a question that was asked repeatedly in Chinese, and when it was finally translated it was this. *At any time during the kidnapping, was I beaten or injured in any way.*

This question was asked, as it had a bearing on the final result of the punishment to be meted out to the three kidnappers on trial. Thankfully for them anyway, the answer was negative.

The final judgment of the court came down almost right away. All three received twenty-year sentences at hard labor to be served somewhere in northern China. I hope they suffered.

The final result did not sit well with me as the other two kidnappers were never apprehended.

I believe the woman was an accomplice but someone's lady friend, so she was not named.

I also believe the Major gave them away on the last day of the kidnapping. He must have still been on active service with the PLA or some other military body. He must have known that the ransom was not forthcoming and decided to give up the others and achieve immunity for himself. He was never mentioned at trial. As soon as he left the place Friday evening, he was never seen again. The rescue happened within a few minutes of his departure.

Here is my reason for saying this. Many months later, while I was still trying to develop my aviation business in China, I was asked to meet a young man at the Kempinski Hotel. He gave Olivia the impression he was an entrepreneur from Canada and wanted to meet me. Since this is a hotel that I was very familiar with and knew many of the concierges and reception staff, I decided this would not be a problem as I would be surrounded by people I knew and felt it would be safe to meet. This was months before the case was scheduled to be heard in court.

The young man I met was a good looking Asian guy in his thirties. He claimed that he was researching a manufacturer for a tabletop game he had invented and was hoping to find one in China. This was his initial introduction, complete with a business card. He was asking me for potential business contacts that he might talk with. We discussed a few companies in general and how difficult it would be to start a business venture in China.

After we talked for almost an hour, he dropped a bombshell in my lap! It absolutely stunned me. He said he was a relative of Albert's family.

He asked me to drop the charges against Albert. When I told him that was never going to happen, he asked me to wait a minute. He left the area where we were sitting, and when he returned, he brought an older woman to meet me. He introduced her as Albert's mother. I was dumbfounded. She held onto my hand and started crying. She also begged me to drop the charges. She said her husband was a retired governor of a province in China, but was now retired and very ill living in Vancouver. He would be devastated if his son was charged with a crime!

I told her in no uncertain terms that I was not going to do anything of the sort. Then the young man surprised me. He brought out an old photograph of a group of soldiers. There were ten uniformed soldiers in the picture. I was able to identify all the kidnappers, including the woman I knew as Yvonne and the Major. He was standing at the end of the row and, quite obviously the officer in command.

I was so upset I walked out of the hotel and never looked back.

This was the end of a sordid tale of deceit, deception, and horrifying experience for me to endure. It has taken me the better part of ten years to get over the disaster I brought on myself.

I retreated to Canada with nothing to show for four years of hard labor, except failed lessons and painful experiences. I hope I learned something from this tragic chapter in my life's journey. Only time will tell.

The end

CPSIA information can be obtained
at www.ICGtesting.com
Printed in the USA
BVHW031140080421
604512BV00005B/43

9 781951 742973